Estate Planning, Life Insurance and Taxes for Canadians

What Insurance Agents Know,
and You Should Know Too — About . . .

Estate Planning, Life Insurance and Taxes for Canadians

OLIVER
PUBLISHING

Estate Planning, Life Insurance and Taxes for Canadians

September 2008

ISBN: 978-1-894749-69-5

With thanks to Helen Piecuch and Dennis Schettler

Publisher: R. Dale Oliver
Writer: Susan Yates
Editor: Patricia Kennedy
Editorial Assistance: Fernanda de̩ Melo
Cover Design: Kitty McKechnie www.kmckecknie.com
Text & Design and Layout: Computer Composition of Canada

Oliver Publishing
151 Bloor Street West, Suite 800
Toronto, Canada M5S 1S4
Tel: (416) 922-9604 Fax : (416) 922-5126
Toll Free 1-800-238-0377
e-mail: info@oliverpublishing.ca
www.oliverpublishing.ca

Printed and bound in Canada

Table of Contents

Introduction

What Your Life Agent Knows

Life insurance suffers from an unfortunate stigma carried over from days past when life insurance agents and used-car salespeople were generally held in the same esteem. The life insurance industry has worked hard to change this perception by raising the educational barre, and now life agents are licensed by the government of the province in which they practise and qualify for their licences after passing a demanding provincially mandated exam and a screening process designed to eliminate those with criminal convictions from entering the profession. After being licensed, agents must complete the continuing-education (CE) requirements prescribed by their province in order to keep their licences. British Columbia is the most rigorous, with a total of 60 years of CE required every two years.

The expertise of life agents naturally centres on life insurance policies, but they are also qualified to sell some investment products, such as annuities and segregated funds. Life agents also sell health insurance, including new insurance products that insurers have recently designed to address the needs of the aging population.

The life insurance industry could also have defeated its reputation—the stigma referred to above—if it had rebranded itself as the risk-management industry. It is the role life insurance fulfils in managing risk, throughout life and especially for retirement and estate planning, that makes it of paramount importance for you as you prepare to retire and live your retirement years to their fullest potential.

Chapter 1

What You Need to Know About Estate Planning

Estate planning is a high falutin' way to describe one very simple thing: making sure your money goes where you want it to go—most efficiently—after your death. You do it to control what happens when you aren't there to speak for yourself, and for this reason, your life insurance agent will tell you that your will is the starting point for estate planning.

Your Will

Incredibly, it is estimated that roughly 50% of Canadians who should have a will don't have one. These people are putting themselves and their nearest and dearest at an emotional and economic disadvantage by failing to execute this vital document.

The Economic and Emotional Costs of Intestacy

When a person dies without a will, he or she is said to die "intestate." Provincial legislation outlines the distribution of assets in the event of intestacy; it varies slightly from province to province. However, in all cases of intestacy where there are no living blood relatives, the estate goes to the provincial government.

That, then, is one economic cost of intestacy. If you have blood relatives but no will, the court will appoint an executor to distribute your assets according to intestacy laws. The assets will be frozen (that is, they will be inaccessible, during the period the executor is in control of the estate). The distribution of the estate will also be significantly delayed.

If the assets are not apportioned among your family in a way they view as fair, the emotional and economic costs to them can be devastating. Potentially, inter-family squabbling, jealousies, and general hard feelings can be your legacy to this and subsequent generations.

Further, you must not assume that your spouse will automatically be your beneficiary. This is simply not true, especially when there are children. However, some provinces will give the spouse an interest in the family home, assign him or her a preferential share of the estate, and provide protection under family law.

Just one reason you need a will.

Naming Your Executor

Another reason the will is important is because it names your choice of executor, the person who will follow the wishes expressed in your will. Often it is family members who are appointed as executors, either singly or jointly, but professionals can also be appointed, such as your lawyer or a trust company.

A fee may be payable to your executor; this is a certainty if you choose a professional. Most provinces set an upper limit of 5% of probatable assets for this fee.

Probatable assets are those assets that are covered in your will and thus will be subject to probate tax. This includes property, cash, investment accounts, and personal property, such as fine art.

If you are thinking of naming your life insurance agent or financial advisor as executor, it is essential for you to find out whether they can fulfil this responsibility; some firms prohibit their agents and advisors from acting as executors.

Preparing Your Will

There are three ways a valid will can be prepared:

- with the aid of a lawyer;
- via preprinted forms available on the Internet, or in kits, usually found at stationers or business-supply shops;
- in your handwriting (known as a *holographic* will).

Lawyers prepare what is typically called a formal or traditional will. It will be prepared in consultation with you and, because it cannot contain any illegalities ("I don't want my husband to get a cent!"), it will usually survive any court challenges to its content. The formal/traditional will must be signed by you and must be witnessed by two people in the presence of each other and of you. Each page should also be initialled by you. Witnesses cannot be a beneficiary or a beneficiary's spouse and must have reached the age of majority.

Traditional wills can be inexpensively prepared for simple estates and provide the least-contestable form of distributing your estate.

Preprinted forms will direct you in filling in the blanks. You should to be very careful, because you won't have the benefit of a pair of expert eyes guiding you or reviewing your decisions.

Handwritten wills must be written entirely in your hand and require no witnesses. Obviously this type of will stands the greatest likelihood of being challenged, particularly if assets are not distributed in the way potential beneficiaries expected or if the rudiments of family law have been broached ("I don't want my wife to get a cent!"). Again, as with the do-it-yourself form, you should exercise great caution.

No matter which type of will you use, it is essential that it addresses all assets and that it does not contain contradictions (for instance, declaring that certain beneficiaries are to share the division of an asset equally, and then naming one of those beneficiaries as the sole inheritor of the asset).

Naming a Beneficiary

The beneficiary is the person or entity who benefits from the assets of the deceased—in other words, the party you want your money to go to. Beneficiaries are named in wills, in insurance policies, and in registered accounts, such as RRSPs and RRIFs.

A beneficiary can be your estate, a person or persons, a class of persons, a charity, or a trustee. Of course, beneficiaries of a will can also fall into any combination of categories in this list.

Naming your estate as beneficiary provides a fund out of which your executor can pay expenses and fulfil bequests. However, an estate can be subject to the claims of your creditors, an issue of particular importance to someone who is a small-business owner at the time of his or her death.

The Issue of Probate

The value of your estate will be subject to probate fees, also called estate administration tax—in essence, a death tax imposed by the province in which you were living when you died. Probate fees are highest in Ontario.

In Ontario, probate fees are not calculated on real property (defined as land and anything of a permanent nature that might be attached to it) outside the province.

The purpose of probate is to prove that your will is valid and that the executor has the authority to transfer assets. Probate fees are based on the value of the assets that are passed through the will. Not all assets must pass through the will. A life insurance agent will tell you that, when you name a person as beneficiary, then the death benefit of your life insurance policy does not become an asset subject to probate. Because the life insurance death benefit passes directly to the person named as the beneficiary of the policy, the value of the death benefit of the policy is effectively increased, because it has bypassed probate. However, if you name your estate as beneficiary, then the proceeds will be subject to probate.

Naming a person or persons as beneficiary of a life insurance policy or RRSP is one strategy that will reduce probate.

Use the chart on page 7 to calculate what you would owe in probate if you were to pass away today. Reducing probate fees is one objective of estate planning and must be addressed when we speak of distributing assets efficiently. If probate can be reduced, why not do so? We will review strategies on reducing probate in the following pages.

When a person is named as beneficiary, they are protected personally from the claims of creditors against the deceased.

Naming a class of beneficiary is relevant when you want to specify a group of people as beneficiaries. Classes may include children and other family relations, such as siblings or grandchildren.

Naming them as a "class" prevents problems if one name is inadvertently left off the list of beneficiaries, or if one named as a beneficiary should die.

There are a number of ways to provide a charitable gift through your will, and making a donation to a favourite charity is an objective of many when planning their estates. Donations made via your will can include cash; a gift in kind, such as a work of art or piece of property; securities, such as publicly traded shares; cultural property; or ecologically sensitive land. There are tax advantages to be gained from leaving a bequest to charity, but it is essential for the charity to be registered with Revenue Canada for these tax breaks to be realized. If you are contemplating a substantial charitable donation upon death, you should seek the advice of an accountant or tax specialist.

Naming a trustee as beneficiary is appropriate when the proceeds are to be managed by one person for the benefit of another. This will be true when the beneficiary has not reached the age of majority, is mentally disabled, or is financially irresponsible.

A beneficiary designation is easily changed by either a new will or an amendment (called a codicil) to an existing will.

Restrictions on Distributing Your Estate

There are very few restrictions on how much you give in your estate and who you can give it to, except:

- a family member (defined by provincial legislation) who is financially dependent on you must be provided for in your will; otherwise he or she may apply to the court to seek support;
- a spouse must be provided for, even if it is at the minimum legal level.

A person who is not competent cannot make a will or alter the terms of a will.

Probate Fees by Province		
BC:	less than $10,000	$0
	$10,001-$25,000	$208
	$25,001-$50,000	$6 for every $1,000
	above $50,000	$14 for every $1,000
AB:	less than $10,000	$25
	$10,000-$24,999	$100
	$25,000-$124,999	$200
	$125,000-$249,999	$300
	above $250,000	$400
SK:	per each $1,000	$7
MB:	less than $10,000	$50 plus
	above $10,000	$6 per $1,000
ON:	less than $50,000	$5 per $1,000
	above $50,000	$15 per $1,000
QC:	notarial will	$0
	other will	$65
NB:	per each $1,000	$5
NS:	less than $10,000	$70
	$10,001-$25,000	$176
	$25,000-$50,000	$293
	$50,000-$100,000	$820
	plus for each additional $1,000	$820 plus $13.85
PEI:	less than $10,000	$50
	$10,001-$25,000	$100
	$25,001-$50,000	$200
	$50,001-$100,000	$400
	plus for each additional $1,000	$4 plus closing fee 0.2%
NF:	less than $1,000	$85 plus
	per each additional $1,000	$5 plus $50
NWT:	less than $10,000	$25
	$10,000-$25,000	$100
	$25,000-$125,000	$200
	$125,000-$250,000	$300
	above $250,000	$400
YK:	less than $25,000	$0
	Above $25,000	$140

ASK YOUR LIFE INSURANCE AGENT

You can also make charitable donations during your lifetime that will provide you with tax advantages while satisfying your desire to contribute to your favourite cause. Life insurance, a charitable annuity, and a charitable insured annuity are some of these gifting vehicles.

Life insurance: You can transfer the ownership of a whole-life insurance policy or universal-life insurance policy to a charity, and name the charity the beneficiary of the policy. The value of your contribution will be the cash surrender value (CSV) of the policy. The amount by which the CSV exceeds the adjusted cost basis will be taxed to you as income, but your contribution will give you a charitable tax credit.

The Adjusted Cost Basis is any change to the book value of an asset resulting from purchases, sales, or any other factors.

Every additional premium payment will be an additional charitable donation, for which you will receive a tax credit.

Charitable annuity: You can donate a lump sum to a charity and then receive an annuity from the charity for the balance of your life. The tax credit in this case is the difference between the lump-sum payment and the market price for an annuity (that is, what you would receive if you were to buy an annuity from an insurer offering the same annual income).

CSV: Cash surrender value is the amount of money the policy owner of a whole-life insurance policy or universal-life insurance policy receives if he or she wants to "cash in" the policy.

Charitable insured annuity: You buy an annuity from an insurer and use some of the annuity payments to pay the premiums on a life policy that names you as the life insured and the charity as the policy owner and beneficiary. The premiums you pay will earn a tax credit, and on your death the charity will receive the insurance-policy death benefit.

An annuity is an investment created by a deposit of capital into an annuity contract. The annuity returns a portion of the capital plus interest on a regular basis (for instance, monthly) to the annuitant (the person who benefits from the contract).

Changing or Replacing a Will

Your will should be reviewed at least every two to three years and updated following all significant events, including the receipt of an inheritance by you, the death of your spouse or separation and divorce, or a change in any of the assets that supported the value of your estate. Or you might simply wish to make a change amongst your beneficiaries.

Your will may be amended by adding or revising clauses (called codicils). These must be witnessed in the same manner as the original will.

If the will is out of date and there are many changes or significant changes, a new will is called for; your new will should state that it revokes and replaces the previous will and any codicils.

A Power of Attorney

We have now seen how the will functions as your voice after you have passed away. However, if sickness or an accident should intervene and prevent you from being able to make decisions or act on your financial obligations, then a power of attorney will act on your behalf.

Just like a will, a power of attorney is a legal document that must be signed by you and witnessed by two people in the presence of each other. In it you appoint someone to look after your financial affairs if you become incapacitated due to sickness, accident, or other mishap. The word "attorney" here should not be confused with a lawyer; the person named as power of attorney can be anyone you choose. Since you are giving this person considerable power, the decision should be made carefully.

A power of attorney for property can be general or limited. A general power of attorney bestows a wide range of rights on the attorney; the attorney is even allowed to borrow money on behalf of the client. A limited power of attorney constrains the actions of the attorney.

As its name implies, a power of attorney for personal care authorizes a person to make personal-care decisions if you become incapacitated.

In Quebec, a power of attorney is called a Mandate Given in Anticipation of Incapacity. The Mandate may grant simple administrative powers (i.e., allow limited investments aimed at preservation of assets), or full administrative powers (i.e., allow a wide range of investments designed to increase assets).

Just as the provincial executor steps in when a will does not exist, so too does the province step in in the form of the provincial public guardian or trustee when you have failed to execute a power of attorney or grant a mandate.

An excellent power-of-attorney kit is available at:
www.attorneygeneral.jus.gov.on.ca/english/family/pgt/poa.pdf

WHAT IS A LIVING WILL?

A living will is also called an advance health-care directive; it can be included in a power of attorney or as a separate document. Living wills are considered to be part of the estate-planning process. Living wills instruct medical practitioners about the type and intensity of medical treatment you want to receive (for instance, special efforts that you may, or may not, want made under certain circumstances).
A living will is an expression of your wishes; it is not binding.

Avoiding the Useless Will

A will that cannot be located when it's needed is not just a source of frustration for those who may be looking for it but, if it cannot be found, will render you intestate.

Make sure your executor knows where you have stored your will; many people do not store it in their homes for fear of fire, water damage, or theft. The probability of these risks should be weighed against the cost and inconvenience of storing it in another location. Many people leave a copy with their lawyer. (A safety-deposit box is not the best place for a will, since your executor will need that will to gain access to your safety-deposit box.)

The disadvantage of having your will in another location is that it is easy to forget about it, thus adhering to the theory of "out of sight, out of mind." You may forget to review it and never get around to making needed changes. Some people find it very effective to set an annual date, such as on a birthday or anniversary, to retrieve and review both their will and their power of attorney.

Let's say you downsize your home, maybe move to a condo. Remember to inform everyone of the new location of the will. If you take it out for review, put it back in the same spot.

Also tell other trusted family members where it is, and remind them—on your annual date of review, for instance—to ensure they haven't forgotten.

Make sure your executor, power of attorney, and trusted family members know the location of your will, power of attorney, and all important documents, such as life insurance policies, mortgage papers, and deeds, as well as a list of financial institutions you deal with.

Chapter 2

The Efficient Distribution of Your Estate

The word "efficiency" is usually used in the context of estates and other financial matters to describe reducing taxes. So, when we speak of distributing your estate efficiently, we mean ensuring that the beneficiaries receive their maximum entitlement and that all necessary taxes are paid—but no more than necessary.

In the previous section we instructed you on how to make sure your money goes where you want it to go. Now let's talk about doing so most efficiently. This process begins during your lifetime, so that, upon your death, your affairs are structured to take advantage of tax rules.

Reducing Probate Expense

There are a number of ways you can beat the taxman when it comes to saving money on probate.

Name a Beneficiary

We began by pointing out that naming a person as beneficiary, where possible—such as in your life insurance policy—thereby removes those assets from the value of the estate. This is an easy step that can mean significant savings during probate.

Give It Away

Another solution for reducing probate seems very straightforward: simply give your assets away during your lifetime. However, be aware that doing so may cause you to incur a capital-gains tax hit, since the asset must be transferred at fair market value.

Fair market value is the price you would get for selling the asset on the open market.

This means, for instance, that if you give away your cottage to your child, in the year the gift is made you would be faced with the following calculation (this may look onerous but the calculation really takes only a simple few steps):

How capital-gains tax is calculated.

Establish the fair market value of cottage:	$250,000
Subtract how much you paid for the cottage (ACB):	$50,000
To arrive at the capital gain on the cottage:	$200,000
Take half the capital gain to determine the taxable capital gain:	$100,000
Determine your marginal tax rate:	44%
Multiply the taxable capital gain by your marginal tax rate to find the amount of the capital-gains tax owing on the cottage:	$44,000

Bear in mind that this is no different than if the cottage is passed by your will to your child, except that probate tax would first have to be paid on the $250,000 before the capital gain is calculated. In the case of gifting, you are incurring the tax bill; after your death; your estate or your beneficiary will incur the tax bill.

In Canada we have a graduated tax rate, so basically the more you earn the more you pay. Your marginal tax rate is the amount of tax you pay on the last dollar added to your taxable income. If you don't know your rate, you can err on the side of caution and use 50%.

You could benefit by waiting. If you give the asset away when you are sixty, chances are your income is still quite high, as is your marginal tax rate. You're going to have to pay a lot of tax on your gift. However, if you give the asset away when you are eighty, you will probably have less income and be in a lower tax bracket, and your marginal tax rate will be correspondingly lower.

A taxable capital gain is half the increase in value of the asset. The capital-gains tax is the taxable capital gain, multiplied by your personal marginal tax rate.

Of course you will have this same benefit if you die at an older age and pass the asset to your beneficiary in your will. Again, your marginal tax rate is probably going to be lower, since you have aged. Let's say it has dropped to 30%. Then taxes on the property with a $100,000 capital gain would be reduced to $30,000. So, waiting or gifting now can be a dicey decision, since no one can predict with any accuracy when they are going to die. It will also depend on whether you have the funds available now to pay such hefty taxes.

Hold Joint Cash Accounts

If you hold cash in a personal account, on your death it will become part of your estate and probate will be paid on the amount in the account. Further, the cash will be tied up through the whole probate process. However, if you have a joint account, the money becomes the property of the other account owner. This not only saves the expense of probate but gives the other account owner continued access to funds that may be necessary at the time of your death.

Consider Owning Assets Jointly

Probate tax may also be reduced by registering assets as joint tenants with rights of survivorship (JTROS). This means the asset has two owners: you and someone else. When you die, the asset automatically becomes the property of the other person and does not pass through your estate. Quebec does not have this form of ownership.

It is not necessary to establish a spouse as a joint tenant, since assets automatically roll over to him or her tax free on your death in any case. However this form of ownership is sometime used with children.

To take advantage of this strategy, it is best if the ownership is established as joint tenants with right of survivorship when the asset is purchased. If an asset is transferred from your ownership to JTROS later, then once again—as in our example above—it will be deemed by Canada Revenue Agency to have been transferred at fair market value. Capital-gains tax here we come! There may also be tax consequences if the joint tenant is not your spouse; get the advice of a tax specialist to ensure you will benefit from using this technique.

Choose a Segregated Fund Investment

Segregated funds are an investment product sold by insurance agents. They have many similarities to mutual funds, and some very distinct differences.

We are going to explore segregated funds elsewhere in this book but, within the context of saving probate fees, you should be aware that segregated-fund contracts are exempt from probate as long as the beneficiary is not the estate.

Segregated funds might be an option for you if you already invest in mutual funds—or are considering doing so. Like mutual funds, segregated funds pool your money with that of other investors. They offer professional management and diversification, and they can be held in registered plans. Unlike mutual funds, segregated funds are sold in a contract that is designed to tie you into the investment for a ten-year term. You can extract yourself from the contract earlier, though there will be hefty penalties to pay. Segregated funds are also unique in that they guarantee the return of principal after the ten-year period.

A segregated fund is an insurance contract, governed by life insurance legislation. This is why, on your death, the value of the seg fund can flow directly to a named beneficiary and bypass probate.

Create a Trust

Another way to dodge probate is to transfer assets to an alter-ego or joint-partner trust if you are sixty-five or older. An alter-ego trust is used by a single person; the joint-partner trust is used when there is a spouse. There is no tax cost to transfer assets into the trust; taxes will be due as you receive income during your lifetime from the trust and the remainder will be taxed at your death (if the assets are in an alter-ego trust) or on the death of the survivor (if they are in a joint-partner trust).

A trust is a legal arrangement in which one or more people who are called the trustees hold legal title of the trust property for the benefit of others, the trust beneficiaries. The person who creates the trust, the trustee, and the beneficiary can be the same person, or different people.

The way the trust works is as follows: with the help of a lawyer you create the legal documents for the trust and transfer assets into the trust. All the capital in the trust and the income it produces is for you, or for you and your spouse, only. You pay tax on the income you receive at the highest marginal tax rate.

The trust can be revoked and it can be changed. If you establish a co-trustee and all your assets are in the trust, you will not need a power of attorney for personal property because your personal property will be within the trust and can be managed by your co-trustee.

A trust can be costly to establish, depending on the complexity of assets being transferred, and there will also be an annual cost to file a tax return on behalf of the trust. Many people with fairly simple estates, or estates without a high value, may find the trust route both too costly and too complex for their needs.

Freeze Your Estate

Estate freezing will freeze the value of "growth assets," so that future asset growth passes to children or a spouse. Growth assets can be shares of a privately held company that your children or spouse intend to keep going, and stocks, bonds, and real estate.

If you freeze an estate, the accrued value of the assets up to the freeze date accrues to you, and subsequent growth accrues to your children or spouse. The value at the freeze date is taxed to you or your estate. Any asset value growth after the date of the freeze will be taxed in the hands of your children or spouse when they die or dispose of the assets.

"Freezing" simply means taking the value of an asset at a point in time and allowing the growth in its value from that point onward to belong to another person.

An estate freeze is very difficult to reverse, and can be very costly. You should consult with an expert before undertaking such a course of action.

A simple estate freeze

A sale or gift of an asset when its value is low can be a simple way of transferring the tax liability of growth.

A not-so-simple estate freeze

The ownership of privately owned companies is structured in such a way as to have common shares and preferred shares. Shares represent the value of the company: a company worth $1 million with 100 common shares has a common-share value of $10,000 each. If the company grows to $2 million, the shares increase in value to $20,000 each.

At any time, common shares in a private company can be exchanged for preferred shares without triggering income tax for the person making the exchange. Just as the value of the common shares will be based on the value of the company, so too will the value of the preferred shares after the exchange has been made.

So, if you are a shareowner in a company who wishes to freeze the growth in your company, you will exchange your common shares for preferred shares, which don't appreciate. Your children can then be issued new common shares, which will have a very low value. As the company grows, the value of the common shares increases while the value of the preferred shares does not change. Thus, future growth accrues to the children, while you can redeem your shares at any time for their original "exchange" value.

The corporation can also continue to provide you with an income, by paying you a salary if you continue to work there, or by paying you dividends.

A Second Will

If you have assets that are not subject to probate, such as shares in a private company, in Ontario you can establish a second will to deal with these assets alone.

If there is any doubt as to whether an asset is subject to probate, it must go into the primary will. If it is included in the secondary will by error, it will then defeat the purpose, because it will make the secondary will subject to probate.

Exchanging Equity for Debt

If you own real estate other than your primary residence, and you have debt, you may want to convert that debt to a charge—such as a mortgage—against the real estate. This will reduce its value for probate.

THE PRIMARY RESIDENCE

Your primary residence is passed to your spouse tax free, and then can be received by your spouse's heirs tax free if they do not already have a principal residence of their own. Your primary residence can be a home—including your cottage, or a condo, or share in a co-op. Each family unit (you, your spouse, and any unmarried children under eighteen) can have only one primary residence at a time.

So, if you own a home and a cottage, and you declare the home as your primary residence, the cottage will become taxable upon your death. If the tax cannot be paid by your estate, the property must be sold. This is how families "lose" properties that have been owned for generations. Further complicating the issue is that, if any of the children do not want the cottage, their share of the estate will still be responsible for a proportional amount of the tax on the capital gains due on the property.

Dealing with capital-gains tax on a cottage is one of the key uses of life insurance that we will discuss later in this book.

Review

Let's review the strategies available to you to reduce probate so the least amount of tax is paid on your final tax return, and the amount your beneficiaries receive is maximized:

- name a beneficiary other than your estate for your life policies, RRSPs, and RRIFs;
- give your assets away while you are alive;
- hold cash in a joint account;
- register assets as joint tenants with rights of survivorship;
- create an alter-ego or joint-partner trust;
- choose a segregated fund for investing;
- freeze your estate;
- use multiple wills to segregate assets;
- take a charge against property to reduce its value.

Anything Else?

If you are the owner of shares of a private Canadian company (officially called a qualified small business corporation), then you are entitled to receive a lifetime capital-gains exemption of $750,000 on the sale of those shares. This sale and the corresponding tax exemption could be received either during your lifetime or if the shares are sold upon your death.

There are a number of restrictions on the definition of a qualified company and the terms that must be met (such as a two-year ownership requirement prior to sale), but this exemption obviously provides a major tax benefit to those who qualify.

For Those with U.S. Property

If you own property in the United States, it will be subject to U.S. federal estate tax. Many states also levy their own taxes. The property will also be subject to Canadian capital-gains tax.

The U.S. estate tax is based on the fair market value of assets, minus certain allowable deductions. The taxable estate is then subjected to the federal estate tax at graduated rates between 18% and 45%.

If the property you owned in the United States was worth more than US$60,000, after your death, a U.S. estate tax return must be filed that discloses all your worldwide assets.

If you qualify for the small-estate exemption, U.S. estate taxes will apply only to U.S. real estate and business assets for Canadians with worldwide assets valued at less than US$2 million in 2008 and $3.5 million in 2009.

However, if you do not qualify for that exemption—in other words, if your total estate is worth more than US$2 million (2008) or $3.5 million (2009)—you will be taxed on your U.S. holdings *as a percentage of your total worldwide assets*. Even if your U.S. holdings are minor in comparison to your total assets, you could face a significant U.S. tax liability.

You will benefit from a tax credit that is increasing until 2010, at which point the U.S. estate tax is repealed for the year. It is then intended to be reinstated in 2011 at a higher rate than for years 2006 through 2010. There is some uncertainty about what will actually occur in 2010 and thereafter.

Some strategies to reduce U.S. estate tax are also available, such as owning U.S. real estate in a Canadian corporation. A Canadian corporation cannot be subjected to U.S. estate taxes. Seek the advice of a U.S. tax specialist before proceeding.

It is generally agreed that a wise strategy is to acquire life insurance in order to pay the U.S. tax if your intention is to continue to hold the asset.

The value of a life insurance policy will be included among your worldwide assets.

Chapter 3

What Happens When You're Gone

Now we've seen many of the ways that you can lower taxes that will be owed in what is ominously called the terminal return—your final tax bill. Preparation of the return is one of the duties your executor will perform or will hire someone to do. What else can be anticipated when all has been said and done?

It's the End of Paying Tax

The filing of your final tax return by your executor is the final chance to try and minimize any taxes that may be due as a result of your passing. Your executor may be required to file up to four income-tax returns after your death. They are due either by April 30 of the year after the year of death or six months after death, whichever is later.

The four returns are:

1. the final personal income tax;
2. the "rights and things" return (see below);
3. the return if you were a partner of proprietor of a business;
4. the return if you were the beneficiary of a trust (not including an alter-ego or joint-partner trust).

The reason separate returns are prepared is to take advantage of tax credits that can be deducted in each of the returns, thus multiplying their effect in reducing taxable income. This includes such credits as the age credit, the basic personal tax credit, and the spousal tax credit. Other credits may only be used in specified returns or may be split between returns.

Your estate is a separate legal entity that must also file annual tax returns each year until all its assets are distributed.

"Rights and things" is money that was owed to the taxpayer at the time of death but had not been received. It can include accrued unpaid vacation benefits for someone that was still working, interest coupons from bonds, and declared but unpaid dividends.

Your estate is also able to make a final contribution to your spouse's RRSP if he or she is less than 71 years of age. If there is unused contribution room in your spouse's plan, it is wise for the estate to make the maximum contribution to receive the maximum deduction.

What Your Spouse Should Expect (or What to Expect When You've Expired)

Your death need not create a tax liability for your spouse; tax laws permit tax-free rollovers to ensure that your spouse's standard of living is not diminished by your death.

Let's take a look at what happens to your assets after death, so that you and your spouse will know where you stand and what should be prepared for.

One of the great benefits of life insurance is that the beneficiary, whether your spouse or another person, receives the money tax free.

Real Property

The principal residence inhabited by you and your spouse will pass to your spouse tax-free. Then, when your spouse dies, the fair market value of the property becomes part of the estate of your deceased spouse. The inheritor receives the property at this value. Subsequent increases in the value of that property become a taxable capital gain when the property is sold, and the inheritor must pay capital-gains tax accordingly.

Other real estate, such as rental property, is considered capital property.

Capital Property

Capital property, also called capital assets, are investments to which capital-gains tax may apply, such as:

- property other than the principal residence;
- stocks;
- bonds;
- mutual funds;
- segregated funds;
- all other forms of investments, such as mortgages;
- jewellery;
- antiques;
- art.

When capital property is left to your spouse in your will, capital-gains tax is deferred until your spouse dies. Just as with the principal residence, it then becomes part of his or her estate and will be passed on through his or her will to a beneficiary.

To ensure that property is not passed on and passed on for eternity without taxes being paid, there cannot be a tax-free rollover to anyone but a spouse. So, when your spouse dies, capital-gains tax will have to be paid by his or her estate before the property is inherited by the beneficiary. If the estate is unable to pay the tax owed, the beneficiary will have to pay the tax or the property will be sold. The executor cannot transfer the property to the beneficiary until the tax bill is cleared.

As we saw earlier, capital-gains tax is determined by the fair market value of the property (today's value in other words), minus its adjusted cost base (the amount you spent to acquire the property), divided in half and then multiplied by your marginal tax rate. Previously, we did the calculation based on the value of a cottage. Now, let's follow the same steps to determine the capital-gains tax on some shares you own.

Let's say you bought 100 shares for $1,000, and on your death they are worth $3,000. The capital gains tax will be $3,000 – $1,000 = $2,000, divided in half = $1,000, multiplied by your marginal tax rate, let's say 30%. The capital-gains tax will be $300.

You and your estate can pay less capital-gains tax if you have capital losses. Capital losses are incurred when the capital property is valued lower than its adjusted cost base. For instance, if you invested in Nortel at $75 per share and it is now worth $10, you have incurred a capital loss of $65 per share. Just as a capital gain is halved, so too is a capital loss. So, using our example, the allowable capital loss would be $32.50.

Because investments don't always increase in value, the capital loss was invented.

During your lifetime, capital losses can be used only to reduce capital gains. They can be carried back three years and forward indefinitely. However, in the year of your death, net capital losses can be used against other income earned that year and the year before.

Your RRSP or RRIF

Your RRSP or RRIF can roll over tax free to your spouse's RRSP (if he or she is younger than 71) or RRIF or that of a child or grandchild who is financially dependent on you due to a physical or mental deformity. You can also roll the funds into an annuity for such a child.

If your plan is locked-in (a LIRA or LRIF) because it was funded with money from a registered pension plan or another locked-in plan, your spouse, a named beneficiary, or your estate will receive the funds that exist in the plan.

The new Life Income Fund introduced in Ontario in 2008 allows your spouse to transfer the full amount in the plan to his or her own RRSP or RRIF as an alternative to receiving the funds if you die. Money held in an LRIF can also be transferred.

If you have named any other beneficiary, an amount equal to the fair market value of all property held in the RRIF at the time of death is considered to have been received immediately before your death. This amount will be included in your terminal tax return so that taxes owing can be calculated and paid before your beneficiary receives the proceeds of the plan.

Cash

As we discussed earlier, cash held in a personal account will become part of your estate and subject to probate fees. But if the account is a joint account, it becomes a personal account of the surviving account owner.

It's a good idea to hold cash in a joint account, so that, if one of the account owners dies, the cash does not become part of the estate of the deceased.

An Inheritance You Received

If you have received an inheritance, you do not need to commingle it with assets you share with your spouse. It can remain separate, for your use and enjoyment only. On your death, it, in turn, can be inherited by another, who may choose to commingle the inheritance with his or her spouse, or not.

Since the inheritance is passed on through the will, it will be subject to probate and possibly other forms of taxation, depending on the form the asset takes. If it is capital property, then there may be capital-gains tax.

Guaranteed Investment Certificates

When a GIC is not held in a registered plan, and is in your name only, it will become an asset of your estate. If it is held with a joint owner, such as your spouse, the GIC will pass to that person.

A registered account is a Registered Retirement Savings Plan or Registered Retirement Income Fund.

In a registered plan, the GIC will pass to the named beneficiary.

Segregated Funds

One of the ways seg funds are different from mutual funds is in the guarantees they provide. There are two guarantees: the maturity guarantee and the death-benefit guarantee. The maturity guarantee provides for the return of at least 75% of deposits ten years after the date the contract has been signed by the investor. Some companies guarantee 100%. The amount that may be received upon maturity is, of course, expected to exceed the deposits, due to investment growth and compounding over the ten-year period.

The death-benefit guarantee also provides a return of at least 75% of deposits and will also be paid whether you own the contract for a day or for ten years minus a day.

When you acquire a segregated-fund contract you are known as the contract holder. You will name an annuitant of the contract who will receive the value of the contract at the end of the ten-year period. You will also name a beneficiary who will receive the value of the contract if you die. If your investment has performed poorly, that amount may be only the guaranteed amount. But, more than likely, given the long-term nature of the investment (ten years), your beneficiary is going to receive an amount greater than the guarantee. How much greater it is will be a function of investment performance.

The beneficiary receives the death-benefit-guarantee amount tax-free. The amount he or she gets over and above the guarantee may be taxed as a capital gain or as income; the insurance company will be able to advise on this issue.

The beneficiary has many options as to how to receive the proceeds. He or she can:

- receive a lump-sum payment;
- leave the amount on deposit and receive interest;
- get monthly installments of a fixed amount;
- take monthly installments for a fixed period;
- decide on a combination of fixed and variable income;
- receive an annuity—either in monthly installments guaranteed for life or as a variable annuity.

Annuities

Annuities are also an investment product typically associated with insurance companies. Only insurance agents can sell life annuities, but term-certain annuities (guaranteeing regular payments for a specific period) are available through other financial institutions, such as banks.

If you die owning a term-certain annuity, its income will be paid either to your estate or to a beneficiary; the beneficiary has two options of how to receive the payments. They are:

- for the balance of the term;
- as a lump sum.

Life annuities come in many different forms. Whether there is a payment to a beneficiary after your death depends on the type of life annuity you held. A straight life annuity makes no payment. If the annuity is a Joint-and-Last-Survivor annuity held by you and your spouse, then your spouse will continue to receive the income for the balance of his or her life. There will be no beneficiary. An installment-refund annuity and a cash-refund annuity will make a payment to a beneficiary; a life annuity with a guaranteed number of payments will make a payment to a beneficiary if you die before the period of time specified in the contract.

You will want to check with your life insurance agent on the tax status of the continued annuity payment to your spouse.

Your Registered Pension Plan

The amount that is received from your pension plan by your spouse or beneficiary after your death depends on whether you were enrolled in a defined-benefit pension plan or a defined-contribution pension plan and whether your death occurs before or after your date of retirement.

Death prior to retirement: Defined-benefit plan

If you die before beginning to receive your monthly retirement benefit, and you were not vested—in other words, if you are not entitled to the contributions your employer made to the plan, because you were enrolled in the pension plan with the employer for less than two years before your death—the value of your plan will consist of your contributions, with interest, to the date of your death. If you made no contributions, the value of the plan may be zero.

A Transfer Value is the amount of an immediate lump-sum payment that is estimated to be equal in value to the future pension payments the member can expect at Normal Retirement. The basis for calculating the Transfer Value is dictated by the Canadian Institute of Actuaries. The interest rates, which are based upon long-term bond rates, are established every month.

If you were vested, your spouse or beneficiaries will be entitled to the commuted value, or Transfer Value, of the pension as of the date of your death. Some plans permit your spouse to convert the Transfer Value to a monthly pension of equal value. The value of the plan can roll over tax free to your spouse's Locked-in Retirement Account (LIRA), or Locked-in RRSP, if he or she is younger than 71. A LIRA was previously known as a Locked-in RRSP. The LIRA is established with the institution of his or her choice. Because it is locked-in, the funds can be withdrawn only for retirement purposes.

Your spouse may also roll over the pension to an annuity.

Death prior to retirement: Defined-contribution plan

As with the defined-benefit plan, the value of your plan is partly a function of whether you and your employer contributed to the plan; if you are not vested, you do not receive the employer contribution and your spouse receives your contributions plus interest. This is called the Account Value.

The Account Value can be received by a spouse or beneficiary on a tax-free basis when it is rolled into a LIRA.

Death after retirement: Defined-benefit plan

The amount to be received by your spouse will be the result of the form of pension you selected with your employer.

If you selected the Normal Form of pension, it is often a single life pension with a guaranteed period based only on your life. This means that, at retirement, you would have received an income for as long as you lived. However, if your death occurs prematurely, a guaranteed number of payments will be received. For example, if the plan provides a life-only pension with a five-year guarantee, and you received 22 monthly payments prior to death, your beneficiary will be paid a commuted value based on 38 payments (60 – 22).

Regulations in many jurisdictions require that a married pensioner must take a Joint-and-Last-Survivor pension **unless** the spouse specifically declines that option in writing when the pension benefit is chosen. If you select the Joint-and-Last-Survivor pension, the amount of pension paid to your spouse will be less than if the amount was paid out to you over the course of your life. The reduction occurs because a joint pension is expected to be paid for a longer period. The younger your spouse, the larger the reduction.

Death after retirement: Defined-contribution plan

Your spouse will receive the Account Value, just as he or she would have done if your death had occurred before retirement. The same restrictions apply on the funds.

Canada Pension Plan/Quebec Pension Plan

If you were a CPP/QPP contributor, a death benefit is payable to your estate. Thus, probate fees will be payable on the benefit.

If there is no estate, payment will be made to the person responsible for funeral expenses, the surviving spouse or common-law partner, or next of kin, in this order.

The benefit is equal to the total payment that would have been received by you over the course of six months at age 65. The maximum death benefit is $2,500. To receive the benefit, your executor must make an application to Human Resources Development Canada.

When a will exists, the executor named in the will must apply for the death benefit within 60 days of your date of death. When a will does not exist, or if application was not made within the 60-day period, an application can be made by:

- the administrator appointed by the Court;
- the person or institution who has paid the funeral expenses (the funeral contract or receipts must accompany the application);
- the surviving spouse or common-law partner;
- your next of kin.

Documents that must accompany the application are: the Application for a Canada Pension Plan Death Benefit, your birth or baptismal certificate, and proof of death. All documents must include your Social Insurance Number.

Proof of death may be submitted as a:

- burial or death certificate;
- certification of death from another country;
- life- or group-insurance claim, with a statement from a medical doctor;
- notorial copy of letters of probate;
- registration of death;
- statement of a medical doctor, coroner, or funeral director;
- notification of death by the chief of national defence staff, or from a public trustee.

Certified photocopies of these documents should be provided; not originals. A document will be certified for free in a Human Resources Development Canada (HRDC) office. Otherwise, any of the following (among others) can certify a document:

- an accountant;
- a dentist, chiropractor, pharmacist, social worker, teacher;
- a lawyer, justice of the peace, notary, commissioner of oaths;
- a doctor;
- a minister of religion;
- a bank manager, police officer, postmaster, professional engineer.

To certify a document, the person doing the certification must compare the original to the photocopy, and provide:

- his or her official position or title;
- his or her signature (also printed);
- his or her phone number;
- the date on which the document was certified;
- a statement as follows: "This photocopy is a true copy of the original document which has not been altered in any way."

Survivor benefits

The Canada Pension Plan/Quebec Pension Plan survivor's pension is paid to your spouse or common-law partner.

A separated spouse may qualify for the benefit if there is no cohabitating common-law partner.

The amount received as a benefit is determined by the age of your survivor, whether he or she is disabled, and whether he or she is raising your dependent child or children.

Your survivor who is 65 or older will receive 60% of your "calculated" retirement pension. The maximum pension for a CPP contributor in 2008 was $884.58.

The Canada Pension Plan children's benefit is paid to your natural or adopted child, or to a child in your care and control at the time of your death. The child must be either under 18 or between the ages of 18 and 25 and in full-time attendance at a school or university.

Old Age Security (OAS)

Your Old Age Security benefit stops upon your death, and neither your spouse nor any other beneficiary can continue to receive your benefit.

Life Insurance

An insurance claim can arise from a:

- life policy;
- group policy;
- health policy.

Life policy

When your life insurance agent learns of your death—if you are the life insured—he or she must supply the person claiming the death benefit with the necessary forms. The agent may assist in completing the forms before he or she submits them to the claims examiner (the person who verifies that the claim is valid) at the insurer's head office.

Whenever a claim is made, the agent or claimant must provide the insurance company with:

- the policy number;
- the name and address of the deceased;
- the date of death and cause (if known);
- the beneficiary's name;
- the name and address of the claimant.

All death claims require a claimant's statement (completed by the person requesting the benefit) and an Attending Physician's Statement (APS) that confirms the date and cause of death. Sometimes, a copy of the death certificate, coroner's report, or provincial medical examiner's report may be required.

Finally, the policy must be returned to the insurer, or a loss-of-policy form must be submitted if the original policy cannot be located.

Claims examiners receive and review the information from the agent, as well as the claims statement, to confirm that:

- the insurance contract was in force when you died;
- you were the life insured;
- the loss is covered by the contract;
- the claimant is the same as that named in the policy.

When satisfied with these details, the examiner calculates the amount to be paid under the claim. This is called the **net death benefit**.

The ***net death benefit*** is the face value of the policy, plus any extras the beneficiary may be entitled to receive. Extras include:

- payments that may be increased by a rider, such as the accidental death benefit;
- unpaid dividends;
- paid-up insurance;
- the account value, if the policy is a universal life contract that has specified a return of the value of the account.

Any outstanding premiums and policy loans, including any interest outstanding on the loan to the date of death, will be subtracted from the policy's face value.

Upon approval of the claim, the insurance company pays the death benefit directly to the beneficiary named in the policy.

Group policy

The amount of death benefit for a group policy will be determined by the benefit schedule of the policy. This schedule can be structured as a stated amount, or as an amount determined by a formula that is linked to your salary if you are the insured (e.g., one times salary).

The beneficiary receives the death benefit in a lump sum.

The claimant will be expected to provide the same documents as are required for a personal-policy death claim.

Health policy

If your death results from an accident for which you were covered by an Accidental Death and Dismemberment policy, then a death benefit will be paid in a lump sum to the beneficiary named in the policy. Again, the same documents must be provided when the claim is made.

AVOIDING THE USELESS POLICY

Just as a will that can't be located is of no use, so too is a life insurance policy of which your executor or the beneficiary of the policy is unaware. Because you are less likely to review or make changes to your policy than you are to a will, and so may be tempted to squirrel it away, think about the probability of someone finding it after you pass away. Make sure such valuable documents can be found easily if you are not around.

Summary of Taxation of Your Assets After Death

Asset	Spouse as Beneficiary	Beneficiary other than spouse
Annuity	Must be taken into income	Must be taken into income
Bonds	Received tax free	Must pay capital-gains tax
Cash	Received tax free, providing account is a joint account	Must be taken into income
CPP	A spouse who is 65 or older will receive 60% of the "calculated" retirement pension of the deceased; otherwise pension benefits are determined by age of spouse, whether he or she is disabled, and whether he or she is raising your dependent children.	Children may receive a benefit if they are under age 18 or are between the ages of 18 and 25 and in full-time attendance at a school or university.
GICs: in non-registered account	Will be received tax free if the account is a joint account	Must be taken into income
GICs: in registered account	Will be received tax free if named as beneficiary	Must be taken into income
Inheritance you received	When not commingled with joint assets, your spouse does not necessarily receive anything. If your spouse does receive the inherited asset or funds on your death, taxes will be owed.	Taxes must be paid according to type of asset: cash will be taxed as income, capital property will be taxed as capital gain.
Life Insurance	Net death benefit received tax free	Net death benefit received tax free
Mutual funds	Received tax free	Must pay capital-gains tax
Old Age Security	No payment made	No payment made

Other real estate	Received tax free	Must pay capital-gains tax
Principal residence	Received tax free	Received tax free if no principal residence owned; otherwise must declare which residence will be principal, sell or rent the other, and pay taxes owed.
Private pension: death after retirement	Certain types of pension income may qualify for the $2,000 income-tax credit.	Certain types of pension income may qualify for the $2,000 income-tax credit
Private pension: death before retirement	Certain types of pension income may qualify for the $2,000 income-tax credit.	Certain types of pension income may qualify for the $2,000 income-tax credit
RRIF	Received tax free into own RRIF	Must be taken into income unless beneficiary is a child or grandchild who is financially dependent on you due to a physical or mental deformity.
RRSP	Received tax free into own RRSP	Must be taken into income unless beneficiary is a child or grandchild who is financially dependent on you due to a physical or mental deformity.
Locked-in RRSP or Locked-in RRIF	Must be taken into income	Must be taken into income
Segregated Funds	Death benefit will be received tax free; account value exceeding death benefit may be taxed as capital gain.	Death benefit will be received tax free; account value exceeding death benefit may be taxed as capital gain.
Stocks	Received tax free	Must pay capital-gains tax

Chapter 4

Legacy Planning: Estate Preservation

To this point you've learned the mechanics of managing your estate and having your affairs in order. Now, let's get to the heart of estate planning—how to make sure the money exists or is found to make your heirs happy! Let's call this legacy planning, geared to preserving the value of the assets you have acquired.

So far we've seen how you can preserve the value of your estate by wise planning around taxes. There are many reasons why you will want to preserve the value of your estate, and they usually revolve around the emotional issues of creating inheritances, whether for your children or others who are near and dear.

There are actually several things to consider around the issue of inheritances: one assumes that your estate is substantial enough to make everyone equally happy (emphasis on equally), but on the other hand, making everyone equally happy may require an estate larger than you are able to leave. If this is so, then estate creation will also be of foremost importance to you. After all, you can't leave behind that which you don't have.

A Note on the Estate

At the end of the day, let's say you want to have an estate, if only for some of the reasons we will discuss, like keeping the family cottage in the family. It is important to understand that an estate is not something that materializes upon your death. Estates are created during your lifetime by saving, investing, and careful spending. They can also be created—or perhaps we should say supplemented—on your death, and we are going to discuss how that can be done in the next chapter.

If the objective is to have an estate, it is very important to review the ways by which estates are depleted, either inadvertently or out of necessity. Some estates that are underfunded (e.g., there is not enough in the estate to pay taxes) are in that state as a result of new rules, regulations, and products that exist within the financial services industry that were not even available for people of your parents' generation (e.g., reverse mortgages).

YOU'VE SEEN THE BUMPER STICKERS

It's not uncommon in communities with a large retired—though typically elderly—population to see bumper stickers trumpeting "I'm Spending My Kids' Inheritance." Do the kids really *expect* to receive an inheritance?

As it turns out, for the most part, no. A study in the United Kingdom found that, whereas almost half the population has inherited something, more than half the population think that they are "not at all" or "not very" likely to receive property as an inheritance in the future, despite the fact that nine out of ten people have the potential to bequeath. This would seem to indicate a significant disconnect between the givers and the receivers.

Two-thirds of those with some potential to leave a bequest say that they will enjoy life and not worry too much about providing an inheritance. Just over a quarter say that they will be careful with their money so that they can leave something. Among the over-eighties, a majority say they will enjoy life rather than worry about leaving an inheritance—proving that there may be a basis in fact for those bumper stickers!

Some groups put much greater emphasis on inheritance. Nearly two-thirds (64%) of Asian people and over half (57%) of Black people with the potential to make bequests say they will be careful with their money for this purpose.

The U.K. study shows that people who are already affluent are most likely to inherit and bequeath substantial amounts. Those who are very poor have very little chance of inheriting, and so will be left further behind. But some of those in the middle will be the first generation in their families to inherit and bequeath.

(Source: *Attitudes to Inheritance in Britain* by Karen Rowlingson and Stephen McKay, Joseph Rowntree Foundation, 2005)

Estate Depletion

Some of the villains in estate depletion are:

- eroding home equity;
- implementation of defined-contribution-plan pensions;
- divorce;
- the changing use of life insurance and viatical settlements (in which companies buy life insurance policies from those who are terminally ill for a percentage of the face value);
- wealth transfer during life;
- health-care costs.

The Erosion of Home Equity

The use of equity in a home to fund expenses has one effect: the value remaining in the home for the purpose of inheritance is decreased. Whether the money is taken as a loan or a reverse mortgage is irrelevant.

Given that the average Canadian senior has over 80% of his or her equity tied up in a house, it is no surprise that reverse mortgages have been increasing in popularity in recent years. You can take out a reverse mortgage when you are as young as 60.

A reverse mortgage is a type of loan that is used to convert the equity in a home into cash. Retirees who find themselves cash poor and house rich can use the money obtained through a reverse mortgage to achieve financial security at the expense of their estate value.

The amount advanced under the mortgage (up to 50% of the home value) depends on the value of the home, your age, and your marital status. The proceeds may be taken as a lump sum, as guaranteed monthly payments, or in a combination of the two.

Essentially, a reverse mortgage is the reverse of a conventional mortgage. Instead of you paying the lender each month, the lender pays you.

The principal amount of the loan, along with accumulated interest, is due when you pass away or sell the home. There is no requirement for monthly repayments, and there is the option of paying off the loan and accumulated interest at an earlier date, along with penalties.

The payments received are taxable, but the interest that accumulates on the loan is tax deductible and usually offsets any tax payable.

Using funds from a reverse mortgage rather than those from an RRSP allows you to take continued advantage of those government plans (e.g., GIS, OAS) that are based on levels of income, since, being tax neutral, reverse mortgages don't raise your income.

Reverse mortgages have legal, appraisal, and closing costs to consider. If interest rates are not fixed, they float and tend to be on the high side. When property values fall, the amount owing on a straight reverse mortgage could exceed the value of the property when sold.

A reverse mortgage has a negative effect on the homeowner's estate value.

THE POWER OF COMPOUNDING

Investors and savers are well acquainted with the power of compounding, and how effectively compounding enhances returns. Here is the reverse of that positive aspect of compounding: if you are only 65 and take $50,000 in a reverse mortgage with an 8% interest rate, and then die at age 88, you will have accumulated $264,677.03 in interest. The total cost to your estate will be $314,677.03, since principal plus interest must be repaid.

Defined-Contribution Plan Pensions

When you join a company with a pension plan, you will typically be offered a pension plan that is either a defined-benefit plan or a defined-contribution plan. Defined-benefit plans are costly for the companies that implement them, because in such a plan the member is guaranteed a certain pension on retirement, and the company must fund the plan so that the member receives what he or she is entitled to receive.

In a defined-contribution plan, the company makes contributions on behalf of the member, but there is no guarantee of how much pension the member will actually receive. The amount of the pension is a result of how well the member invests the contributions to his or her plan. Companies love defined-contribution pensions because they are off the hook when it comes to the value of the pension upon retirement, and they have been moving from defined-benefit plans to defined-contribution plans in droves.

The defined-contribution plan places complete responsibility for the amount of pension on the shoulders of the members. The company still makes a contribution to the pension plan, and sometimes the individual members contribute too. The members must make investment decisions about how to invest the money during the period of accumulation, whether and how much of their own money to add to the company contribution, when to switch investments, and how to allocate investments based on their age, time horizon, and risk tolerance. In other words, they become their own investment advisors—without the benefit of the specialized training that actual advisors must receive.

> The time horizon is the length of the investment period before the funds are needed. If you are 60 and plan to retire at 63, you have a three-year time horizon to retirement.

And, while it is true that the companies perfunctorily educate their members about what they need to know, it is also true that most members do not have the education, knowledge, or confidence to make these very important decisions. As a consequence, over half the members of defined-contribution plans make the default investment choice: a money-market mutual fund that pays no better returns than a savings account but stacks on fees regardless. Many members of defined-contribution plans simply fail to understand how small their pension will be, and they are shocked when they discover the sad truth. Alas, it is then too late to act.

Defined-contribution plan members often end up with lower pensions than their defined-benefit brothers. A lower pension may mean other assets have to be cashed in to provide a retirement income, and thereby the value of the estate will be diminished.

It is also not unreasonable to see how a lower pension and a reverse mortgage could work in tandem to magnify estate depletion.

Divorce

Divorce in your parents' day was a relatively rare event in Canada, and extremely rare in the days of your grandparents. Statistics Canada figures for 2005 show that about 38% of marriages will end up in divorce (about 70,800 divorces total). In 1921, in all of Canada, there were 558 divorces, and in 1961, 6,563.

When children are involved, divorce results in the expense of maintaining two households, until one of the spouses is alleviated from alimony and child-maintenance costs, usually because the other spouse remarries or because the child reaches an age and stage when payments are no longer required. Alimony and child maintenance eat into the money available for saving and investing by the paying spouse. This leaves less "at the end of the day."

It is also a sad fact that only about 50% of the children of divorced couples maintain an ongoing relationship with both parents. Obviously these children are unlikely to benefit from the estate of the parent from which they are estranged.

The Changing Use of Life Insurance and the Dreaded Viatical Settlements

In your parents' day, it was pretty much assumed everyone had a life insurance policy to pay funeral expenses. More recently, people readily acquired term life insurance policies in order to benefit from their very high amounts of coverage at very affordable rates.

The problem with both of these products is that they do very little to enhance the value of the estate. Some money may be saved that would have to have been spent on a funeral, but typically, after children are grown, term life insurance policies are ended, leaving no life insurance in the estate.

Those who do maintain life insurance during their lives may access a product called a viatical settlement. Viatical settlements have been created to relieve people of their life insurance policies in exchange for cash. A viatical settlement allows a person to invest in your life insurance policy, paying mere cents on the dollar value it is worth. When you die, the investor collects the death benefit.

> A viatical settlement transfers the death benefit of your insurance policy to an investor, who pays you a small percentage of the death benefit in cash when the policy is transferred.

It is difficult not to be judgmental about such a product, since when there is dire need and no other recourse to funds, a viatical settlement may be the last chance for immediate money in hand. Let's simply summarize by saying that such settlements obviously drain the value of the death benefit of the insurance policy from the estate.

> Viatical settlements are based on the worth of permanent insurance policies—either whole-life insurance or universal-life insurance.

Wealth Transfer During Life

Wealth transfer during life is a long-winded way to describe gifting. It is not unusual now for grandparents to help pay their grandchildren's higher-education costs or for parents to lay out funds to help children build down payments or bail them out of many types of financial emergencies.

As we said earlier, giving it away during your lifetime has the benefit of reducing the cash in the estate on which probate must be paid, but the disadvantage of such generosity is that the estate value is diminished.

Health-Care Costs

The greatest threat to your wealth is your health. (Thanks to Karen Wernham, CFP™ from RBC Dominion Securities in Newmarket, ON, for that brilliant summary.) We can be thankful for our government health-care plans, but they go only so far in covering costs, and they go almost nowhere in replacing income that may be lost due to sickness or an accident.

Your estate can be ravaged by expenses incurred during your working years because of the costs of disability, of life-threatening illness, of long-term care as you age, and of health care you might incur if you travel or live abroad. Each of these deserves considerable attention.

While you are working

If your income stops while you are working, other assets may have to be used to pay the bills. While government programs in the form of Employment Insurance or the Canada Pension Plan may assist if you satisfy their definition of sickness or disability, their benefit amounts are not designed to sustain a family at the standard of living that was enjoyed prior to the disability.

Disability insurance will replace your income in the event that you become physically or mentally unable to work. Although it gets less attention than life insurance, experts agree that disability coverage is actually more important—especially when statistics reveal that the probability of being disabled is much greater than the chance of premature death.

Your estate will shrink as you use assets to replace lost income.

While many people are covered for the medical costs of severe injury or sickness through health insurance, without disability insurance they are not prepared for the loss of wages that accompanies such a tragedy. In general, if you count on your job to pay the daily costs of living, you should seriously consider disability coverage.

Disability coverage is available through a personal policy or in group policies, usually made available by an employer. Policies are available only to age 65, and to qualify you must work full-time.

The amount of insurance you will receive will be limited to 60% of your regular earned income. This is income that results from activity, such as your salary or money you make from a business you might have. It is not based on passive forms of income, that is, income you would receive whether you were able to work or not. Investment income is the best example of passive income.

A brilliant feature of disability income insurance is that, even though you will receive only 60% of what you earned, it will be tax free.

Your condition must be such that you are under the care of a doctor. Some policies ask that you be unable to perform the essential duties of your own—or regular—occupation. Others can insist that you be unable to perform *any* occupation.

After you have satisfied the definition of disability in your policy, you will receive your disability benefit on a monthly basis for the duration of your benefit period (most commonly two years, five years, or to age 65)—or you will get well and go back to work.

ASK YOUR LIFE INSURANCE AGENT

Disability income policies are very complex: there are five different types of policies and many choices you must make to ensure the policy fits your needs. The premium you pay will be a result of:

- the definition of disability in the policy;
- the duration of benefit payments;
- how long you will have to wait after you have been disabled for the benefit to begin;
- how long total disability must exist before a partial benefit is paid;
- how much will be paid as a benefit.

There are also riders that can be added to the policy. Make sure you find out about the waiver-of-premium rider that will kick in to pay the premiums on the policy if you are receiving a disability benefit.

Life-threatening illness

Due to our increasing longevity, the number of people suffering serious illness is on the rise. Cancer, heart disease, and stroke are affecting an ever-greater number of lives.

The onset of such disease can not only stop your ability to earn an income, if you are still working, but can bring additional expense in the form of home health care, medical devices, or the replacement of the services provided by the patient when he or she was a caregiver to children or aged parents. These expenses can have a significant and long-lasting effect on the estate.

In answer to this need, the life insurance industry introduced a new product called critical illness insurance (CII). A CII policy pays a lump-sum benefit to you if you are diagnosed with any critical illness covered in the policy and, for most conditions covered, if you are still living 30 days after the diagnosis.

Note that you must be living 30 days after the diagnosis for the policy to pay its benefit.

The benefit may be used in whatever way you wish. It can be used to fulfil "dreams" (that always-wished-for trip or holiday) or for more practical purposes (retrofitting a vehicle or the home), or to buy health services through a private health-care system, such as that available in the United States.

Pre-existing conditions are excluded, and payment may not be made in the case of illness or injury due to personal choice (e.g., HIV/AIDS, living in a dangerous area, etc.)

Premiums are based on:

- your age;
- the amount of coverage;
- your gender;
- whether you are a smoker or not;
- the renewability of the policy;
- definitions used within the policy.

All policies cover the top four health conditions: heart attack, cancer, stroke, and heart bypass surgery. Thereafter, up to 23 other illnesses and conditions can be covered. However, there will be differences between insurers on the definitions of the illness covered, and the definition must be satisfied or you will be unable to make a successful claim.

It would be tragic for you to suffer a type of cancer not covered in the policy and find that your CII policy would not make the anticipated payment.

Cancer is an excellent case in point. Many people diagnosed with many types of cancer recover, yet there are others that are terminal. Therefore, the coverage for cancer in the policy must list the types of cancer covered and the impact the cancer must have on the insured before a benefit is paid.

Thus, very specific definitions of the nature and scope of conditions covered will demand a higher premium than definitions that are vague and less likely to be satisfied when a condition occurs.

Here are some examples of how the top four conditions will have to be satisfied:

Heart attack: an acute episode of heart disease due to insufficient blood supply to the heart muscle, especially when caused by a coronary thrombosis or coronary occlusion. Therefore, it is clear the heart muscle must be affected for a claim to be successful.

Cancer: a malignant tumour of potentially unlimited growth that expands locally by invasion and systematically by metastasis. However, some cancers are readily treatable and even cancers such as breast cancer or prostate cancer are not necessarily fatal. There could be a delay before payment is made while the insurance company determines the severity of the cancer and the prognosis for the patient.

Stroke: a sudden diminution or loss of consciousness, sensation, and voluntary motion caused by a rupture or an obstruction, by a blood clot, of an artery of the brain.

Strokes have many degrees of severity, and that severity would have to be established for a claim.

Heart Bypass Surgery: a surgical procedure to bypass blocked heart arteries with a graft. Since surgery is specified in the definition, less-invasive procedures, such as balloon angioplasty, would not qualify for a claim.

Other conditions: Policies can be structured to provide benefits for the following conditions:

- blindness;
- deafness;

- kidney failure;
- major organ transplants;
- multiple sclerosis;
- paralysis;
- coma;
- others, particular to each insurer.

A return-of-premiums rider to this policy will refund premiums if a claim is not made within a specified period of time.

ASK YOUR LIFE INSURANCE AGENT

Ask your agent about the four types of critical illness insurance policies, and the two premium options.

Long-term care

As you are undoubtedly aware, and as we have remarked above, people are living longer—and not just a little longer but, for the most part, much longer. Today, there are about 430,000 Canadians over 85 years old, twice as many as in 1981 and 20 times the number as in 1921. Further, you are part of a generation that has valued its independence and its freedom to make choices. It is unlikely that will change as you age. This means you are going to need money—and lots of it—if your plan is to continue to live independently for as long as possible, and then enjoy a standard of care that is better than that offered by public nursing homes and similar facilities.

Most people grossly underestimate the cost for care in their senior years: private nursing-home care ranges in cost between $40,000 and $70,000 annually. (Even public, subsidized homes can cost upwards of $20,000 per year.) Before that point you may choose to have home care. Currently the cost for home care is about $200/day; in ten years, with an inflation rate of 4%, that cost will be $296/day. Start adding the cost of home care for . . . let's take a conservative estimate of ten years (say, from age 78 to 88) . . . and then ten years of nursing-home care at $70,000 per year, and you can see that a staggering amount of money will be required. And remember to multiply that times two, unless you have other plans for your spouse!

Fortunately the insurance industry has also recently recognized this need and brought forward long-term-care insurance as an alternative to depleting your estate to pay for these costs.

A long-term-care policy can provide peace of mind by assuring you that you can afford necessary care and it will be provided. It's a good idea for you, and might also be a good idea to explore for your parents to preserve their estate value.

A policy can be structured to provide benefits for:

- home health care, also called attendance care, for those expenses that would be incurred by someone who continues to live independently;
- chronic-care for the expense of care in a chronic-care facility, i.e., nursing home;
- medical equipment;
- respite care;
- hospice care;
- adult day-care.

Long-term care is also available as a rider to a life policy.

Benefits

After a period during which the benefit is not paid (called the elimination period), which ranges from zero to 180 days, benefits for long-term-care insurance are paid weekly or monthly. Benefits are payable if there is:

- cognitive impairment: an inability to think, perceive, reason, or remember;

- inability to perform, unaided, two of the five activities of daily living (called ADLs): bathing, eating, dressing, toileting, or transferring positions of the body.

Activities of Daily Living, or ADLs, include bathing, eating, dressing, toileting, and transferring positions of the body. The inability to perform any two of these activities qualifies the insured for the long-term-care benefit.

Money will be paid by the policy for a period as short as three years up to the time of death. This is a detail to sort out between you and your insurance agent.

Terms

The policy is guaranteed to be renewable, and premiums are level for the duration of the policy, including renewal periods. To qualify for a policy you must be between the ages of 31 and 80 (depending on the insurer). Premiums become expensive with age, so the policy should be taken out well before you may need it. There is a 10-day rescission period—that is, you have 10 days after you receive the policy in which you can change your mind and will receive back from the insurer the initial premium you paid when you applied. Of course, you can change your mind at any time about the policy and stop paying the premium. You will not receive back the premiums you paid, and of course you will not receive a benefit.

A waiver of premium transfers the payment of the premium to the insurer once benefits are received by the insured for a specified period of time. This means that, if you start to receive a benefit from your policy, after, say, three months have passed, you no longer pay the premium but the insurer pays it on your behalf.

Riders are available to ensure inflation protection, waiver of premium, and return of premium. Inflation protection is very important in today's climate, in which it is not unusual for people to live many years in a care facility. During that time, the cost of care will increase, at a minimum to keep up with inflation. It is very important that your benefit keeps pace with such increases.

A return-of-premium rider will refund premiums to you under certain conditions.

Limitations

Benefits will not be paid when there is a pre-existing condition, unless care begins at least six months after the policy takes effect.

ASK YOUR LIFE INSURANCE AGENT

All indications are that the cost of critical-illness insurance and long-term-care insurance are going to begin to rise dramatically once the baby boomers start reaching 65 en masse, about 2010, and realize their need for these products. Ask your life insurance agent for quotes now if you are even somewhat concerned about whether your estate could afford these costs or if preservation of its value is an issue of importance to you.

Health care outside Canada

We've all heard the horror stories about the poor shmuck who had a heart attack in Miami and the hospital bill was $30,000 a day. Even though these stories may be exaggerated, they have a basis in fact. Medical expenses outside Canada are very expensive. Very few other single expenses could erase the value of your estate faster than emergency medical treatment outside Canada. You need private health insurance when you are travelling or temporarily living abroad.

Provincial health plans provide very limited coverage, and we urge you to check what your province offers. To give you an idea of just how low "limited coverage" is, here is an overview of what is provided by the Ontario Health Insurance Plan (OHIP).

OHIP funding is designed to cover medical treatment of insured residents of Ontario if they incur an injury or develop a disease while they are outside of Canada. If the illness, disease, condition, or injury arose before you left Canada and it was not treated, or if it is not acute or unexpected, no payment will be made.

OHIP will pay only for insured, emergency, out-of-country health services that are rendered to an insured person. To qualify as an "emergency," your health crisis must meet the following conditions:

- the treatment must be medically necessary; **and**
- the treatment must be performed at a licensed hospital or licensed health facility; **and**
- the treatment must be rendered in relation to an illness, disease, condition, or injury that :
  - is acute and unexpected; **and**
  - arose outside of Canada; **and**
  - requires immediate treatment.

OHIP will not pay more than the service would have cost in Ontario.

For physician services, OHIP will pay the actual cost billed by the out-of-country physician(s) or the cost of the same physician service(s) in Ontario, *whichever is less.* Physician services in Ontario are usually rendered at a significantly lower cost than those billed by out-of-country health facilities.

For health-facility services, OHIP will pay CDN $50 per day.

For in-patient services, OHIP will pay CDN $200 per day. If the services are in-patient services rendered in an operating room, coronary-care unit, intensive-care unit, or neonatal or pediatric special-care unit, then OHIP will pay at the higher rate of CDN $400 per day.

OHIP does not pay for ambulance services, transportation costs, or out-of-hospital food, accommodation, or prescriptions.

Private health-insurance plans are typically designed to provide $5 million in coverage plus a full suite of benefits for you and your spouse. There is no denying the premiums become quite expensive with age, but the alternative is far more costly.

What You Can Do

You know what they say about the weather: everyone talks about it but nobody does anything about it. Don't feel that way about all these factors of estate erosion that we have discussed. You can positively affect the value of your estate; lifestyle changes may be called for, but the decision is yours as to whether you implement change or, alternatively, live the life of the guy who is driving the car with the bumper sticker about spending his kids' inheritance.

Consider:

- Selling your home and downsizing, instead of taking a reverse mortgage.
- Actively managing your defined-contribution plan. If you feel inadequate to make the investing decisions, hire a financial advisor on a fee-for-service basis to consult with you and make recommendations.
- Looking for other sources of income before taking a viatical settlement. You may have another asset that would not have to be sold at the discount that your life policy would be. A reverse mortgage would be a better choice for putting money in your hands.
- Gifting equally. There's no harm in giving away your assets during your lifetime. If your intention in your will was to treat all your beneficiaries equally, then you can ensure you do that with your gifts of assets. The end result will be the same.
- Buying long-term-care insurance for you and your spouse with a return-of-premium rider, so you'll get your money back if you don't need the insurance—and with protection against inflation.
- Buying private health insurance every single time you or your spouse travels outside the country.

Chapter 5

Legacy Planning: Estate Creation

We've seen now how you can take steps to preserve the value of your estate. That being said, the possibility still exists for an estate to be underfunded on the final death of you and your spouse. You can estimate where you stand by looking at your assets and where you want them to go. We've shown you how your capital property and other assets that you own are taxed. If you find, or suspect, a shortfall between what your estate can afford and what you had planned for bequests, then it may be time for you to consider means by which estates are created, or supplemented.

There are several common issues that underlie the need for estate creation. One is the desire to keep a cottage in the family and the other is equalizing bequests. There can be a definite overlap between these objectives.

The Cottage: An Emotional and Expensive Asset

One of the single largest issues for many families is that of the cottage (really the second property of whatever type: ski chalet, family farmhouse, or any property that is not your principal residence) and the capital-gains tax that will be due when it is inherited by those other than your spouse. With recently skyrocketing property values making good properties harder and harder to find and the emotional ties most families develop to their cottage, there are good reasons to ensure it stays within the family, if that is what the family wants.

Your first task is to make sure the family does indeed want to keep the property, and that they have the financial resources to maintain it. There isn't much point in going to the expense of paying those capital gains if the family is going to have to sell it because they can't afford the upkeep.

Life insurance provides a tidy solution to this problem.

For estate-planning purposes, only permanent life insurance must be used. In the next chapter we will review the best types of policies for estate planning.

Let's do an overview of the cottage issue: on the death of you or your spouse (whomever dies last), your cottage, as your second and non-principal, residence, will be taxed as capital property to your estate. The beneficiaries of the property, let's say your children, want to keep the property and can pay the capital-gains tax if they are able. To give them that ability, you will take out a life insurance policy with a death benefit equal to what you estimate the capital-gains tax will be when the property is to be inherited. You will want to take into consideration your current age, the potential increase in value of properties similar to yours, its location, and what the marginal tax rate is likely to be at the time of the death of the last of you and your spouse.

> Your life agent is trained and equipped with software to help you with such calculations.

In every life insurance policy there is a policy owner, a life insured, a beneficiary, a premium, and a death benefit. The policy owner "owns" the policy and is responsible for making the premium payments. The life insured is the person whose death triggers the payment of the death benefit. The beneficiary receives the death benefit. The premium is the cost of the insurance, and the death benefit is the amount of money the beneficiary receives.

If you are younger, and your premium cost is lower, you might choose to prepay the premium for the policy, or perhaps ask your children to contribute to that expense. In that case there will be no further premium payments required. You will acquire a joint-last-to-die policy with your spouse; when the last of you dies, the death benefit is paid. Your children are named as beneficiaries, and when they receive the death benefit from the policy, they use the money to pay the capital-gains tax.

Alternatively, if you are older, and the premium expense is consequently that much higher, you may choose a regular series of premium payments. It won't in the long run be cheaper, since the actuaries at the life insurance company will have very carefully calculated your life expectancy. It may simply be less painful to pay the premium this way. You still structure the policy as a joint-last-to-die. If you are going to pay the premiums, you will be the policy owner. However, you could also make the children the policy owners, in which case responsibility for the premium is theirs. They can still be named beneficiaries.

These scenarios work beautifully, providing every child agrees to own the cottage with the others equally. Problems arise when one child or more wants to opt out. They don't want the property; they'd rather have the money. Now what?

If you have paid the premium expense for the insurance to pay the capital-gains tax on the cottage, those children who are sharing the property will receive the fair market value of that property. Even though the capital-gains tax is much lower than the fair market value, the children are free to keep the property or sell it. If they sell it, they receive the fair market value as theirs.

Difficult decisions may have to be made during your lifetime.

If the children who want the property have paid the premium, you should try to get consensus from the all the children as to how to establish the value of what they are receiving: the cost of the capital-gains tax or the fair market value of the property. Either way you will divide that amount by the number of beneficiaries and then increase the death benefit proportionately by that amount to cover the beneficiaries who do not want to share in the property. For instance, if the capital-gains tax on the property is estimated to be $100,000, and there are two children out of four who want to keep the property, they each need to receive $50,000. The other two children will also need to receive $50,000 to do with as they please. Thus the insurance policy should carry a death benefit of $200,000 total.

If the fair market value is determined as the value of the inheritance, then the two inheriting children will each receive their $50,000, and the other two will receive an amount equal to the fair market value divided by two. The death benefit will be much higher if it is based on the fair market value than if based on the amount of capital-gains tax that will be due.

This provides a true equalization of the estate.

Equalizing the Estate

Another way the estate can be equalized is to dole out assets so that each child or inheritor receives an equal amount, though the assets they receive might be different. Under this scenario, one child might get a stock portfolio, another receives the cottage, and the third the collection of A.Y. Jackson prints. The value of all the assets is equal.

Equalization can be a particularly thorny issue when a family business is involved. As with the cottage, it is a fairly simple matter to resolve if all the children want to be involved in the business or if none of the children want to be involved. If everyone "buys in," an estate freeze like the one we discussed earlier can be very effective. Otherwise, a form of business insurance based on a buy-sell agreement may be the better answer.

> A buy-sell agreement sets out the terms and conditions under which your shares will be bought by your children.

The buy-sell agreement is fundamental to the passing of the business interest, because it sets the terms for the buying and selling of the private corporate shares that you own as a business owner.

The clauses of the buy-sell agreement spell out the parties to the agreement; the contract then details the purpose of the agreement and the requirement for the children who are interested in continuing the business to purchase your shares.

You should take care to append to the agreement a list of the assets of the business that are to accompany the shares being sold to avoid dispute. This list should be reviewed frequently and amended as necessary.

Insurance is placed on your life, as shareowner of the business, for the value of the shares you own, naming the children as beneficiaries. Upon your death, the shares will revert to the corporation, at which point they can be bought by your children using the benefit received from the life insurance policy.

If none of the children wish to inherit any part of the business, insurance can be put in place to help a key employee buy the shares or to have the shares revert to corporate ownership. All these options can be reviewed in depth with your life agent.

Chapter 6

Life Insurance for Estate Planning

Term life insurance has no place in estate planning, because you just never know when your time might be up. Estate planning demands permanent life insurance, insurance that will be there whenever you die.

The Forms of Permanent Life Insurance

There are three forms of permanent life insurance:

- term-to-100 insurance
- whole-life insurance
- universal-life insurance

Each form offers features distinct from the others. The following is an overview of the features and benefits of each that you can discuss in detail with your life agent to find the policy that best suits you.

Term-to-100 Insurance (T-100)

This form of life insurance is fairly described as being "stripped down"; it does not have many of the frills of the other forms of permanent insurance. What it does is provide you with life insurance up to age 100, at which point it either pays out the death benefit or is considered paid up, which means that future premiums are not required to keep the policy in force.

Premiums for T-100 are lower than other forms of permanent life insurance, and it is a perfectly satisfactory choice for estate-planning purposes.

Insured Annuity

An insured annuity is essentially a prescribed life annuity and a term-to-100 life insurance policy, purchased together. The combination of the benefits provided by these products is ideal for those seeking guaranteed income and the preservation of their capital.

Term-to-100 life insurance is a permanent policy that will be in force until you die. It is the least expensive form of permanent insurance.

How an insured annuity works

Using your capital, you buy a life annuity and at the same time take out a term-to-100 life insurance policy with a death benefit equal to the value of the life annuity. So, if you used $500,000 to buy the life annuity, the insurance policy will have a $500,000 death benefit. You receive a guaranteed income stream and use a portion of the regular annuity payments to pay the premiums on the life insurance policy. Upon your death, the death benefit of the life insurance policy is paid directly to your named beneficiary—tax free.

Even if you have health-related issues that drive up the cost of the premiums on the life insurance, there is a balance, because, for the very same reason, your annuity payment will be higher because your life expectancy is lower.

Whole-Life Insurance

Whole-life insurance provides the frills that Term-to-100 doesn't, but at the cost of premiums higher than a T-100.

You pay for policy extras with higher premiums.

In pure whole-life insurance, premiums are paid until you, as the life insured, die. Limited-payment life is a variation, in which premiums are paid over a period of time or to a specified age. For instance, a 20-pay-life policy requires premiums to be paid for 20 years. The coverage however is life-long.

There are several features of both forms of whole-life insurance that can benefit you as the policy owner during your life. They are the policy reserve and policy dividends.

The policy reserve

During the early years of a whole-life policy, you as the policy owner will pay more in premiums than your coverage requires. This creates a "policy reserve." The policy reserve, or cash reserve, increases with every premium payment and by compound growth on the savings within the reserve.

The policy reserve also provides you with the ability to:

- cash in the value of the policy and take the cash surrender value;
- borrow from the cash surrender value via a policy loan;
- use a non-forfeiture option.

Cash surrender value

As you pay premiums and they accumulate interest, a cash value is built in the policy. If you no longer want insurance coverage, then you can receive part of the value of the policy reserve via the policy's cash surrender value (CSV). Cash surrender value is exactly what it says: cash paid to you in return for the surrender of the policy. Thus, unlike the case in term insurance, you receive "money back" if the policy is discontinued.

There is a tax consequence to taking the CSV based on what the adjusted cost basis of the policy is. This is best determined with your life agent.

Taking a policy loan

Up to 90% of the CSV of a policy can be borrowed by you from the insurer in a policy loan. Interest on the loan is charged at the rate specified by the insurer, which is usually competitive with the rates offered by banks or other lending institutions.

If you die before the loan is repaid, the outstanding amount of the loan, plus interest, is deducted from the death benefit. It is possible, therefore, to seriously erode the value of the death benefit with a large loan.

The policy loan can also have tax consequences that you should investigate before taking the loan.

Converting the CSV into non-forfeiture options

Non-forfeiture options give you some alternatives to surrendering your policy in order to continue to enjoy insurance coverage. There are three non-forfeiture options:

- an automatic premium loan (called APL);
- extended term insurance (called ETI);
- reduced paid-up insurance (called RPU).

Non-forfeiture options are simply ways for you to continue insurance coverage, either temporarily when you forget to pay the premium (APL) or through other forms of life insurance (ETI and RPU).

Automatic premium loan (APL):

When you forget to pay the premium or are short of money when the premium is due, the policy will remain in force if you use an automatic premium loan. The APL automatically—without interference by you—charges unpaid premiums as a policy loan against the cash surrender value of the policy in order to continue insurance coverage. It can be used until you recommence premium payments or until the amount of the loan plus interest equals the cash surrender value of the policy. Coverage will end after the grace period, when premiums are no longer paid either by the APL or the policy owner.

The grace period is the length of time—either 30 or 31 days—that elapses after the premium due date.

Extended Term Insurance (ETI):

If you stop paying premiums for whatever reason—this option allows you to keep coverage in force by using the cash surrender value of the policy as a lump-sum premium to buy term insurance. The face amount of the term policy that is acquired will be the *same* as that of the whole-life policy; however, its term will be based on the age that has been attained by the insured when this option is selected. Riders and other benefits from the original policy will be cancelled.

Reduced Paid-up Insurance (RPU):

Whereas ETI uses cash surrender value to switch permanent coverage to term coverage, RPU uses cash surrender value as a lump-sum premium for a whole-life policy that is paid up. You sacrifice the amount of coverage that you had previously for a lesser face amount.

"Paid up" means that no more premiums are required to keep the policy in force.

The new face amount will be based on your attained age and the cash surrender value in the policy.

RPU provides many of the features of the original whole-life policy, including a cash surrender value and insurance coverage for the lifetime of the insured. Dividends, however, are not received, and riders and other benefits are cancelled.

Policy dividends

A whole-life policy can be either a participating policy (called a par policy) or a non-participating policy (called a non-par policy). A participating policy pays policy *dividends*, whereas a non-participating policy does not.

Many people are familiar with the dividends that can be paid as a result of investing in stocks. They are a way for an investor to share in the profits of the company.

Policy dividends paid by an insurer are different. They are not a share of the insurer's profits but a distribution of surplus earnings (i.e., policy overpayments) held in the participating account established by the insurer.

Policy dividends are actually a refund of premium overpayment.

A surplus is created when the insurer incorrectly overestimates mortality rates and expenses, and/or underestimates its investment earnings. It is mandatory for the insurer to keep reserves to meet its insurance obligations, but once those reserves are exceeded, the excess is distributed to the par policy owners as a dividend.

Dividends are not guaranteed, and their amount can vary year-to-year. They begin at the end of the first year of a policy and are paid after the first premium in the second year has been received by the insurer. A key benefit of dividends is that they build inflation protection into the death benefit, since they cause the death benefit to grow—providing they are saved or reinvested in the policy.

Reinvesting dividends builds inflation protection into the policy, since the death benefit will increase.

When you complete the application for insurance, you must indicate how the policy dividends will be received. There are three basic purposes to which policy dividends can be put:

- as savings;
- to acquire more life insurance;
- to reduce premiums.

Dividends as Savings:

The savings option will see policy dividends paid:

- by cheque once a year;
- into a deposit account with the insurer to accumulate interest;
- into a segregated fund.

Dividends Used for More Life Insurance:

You can select:

- paid-up additions (PUAs);
- special term additions (also known as the fifth-dividend option);
- term additions.

A *paid-up addition (PUA)* uses policy dividends to buy additional paid-up insurance. As its name suggests, this paid-up insurance—which is usually a participating policy (par policy) in its own right, with its own cash surrender value—is an addition to the basic policy (hence, paid-up addition). It grows in value annually. A medical exam is not required in order to purchase paid-up additions.

Paid-up additions can increase the death benefit, cash surrender value, and loan value of the policy. Also, they can be surrendered individually each year without affecting the actual policy and received as cash or used to pay premiums.

A *special term addition* is a one-year non-renewable term policy that is typically equal to the cash surrender value of the policy at the end of that policy year. The difference between the cost of term insurance and the policy dividend is paid in cash.

A *term addition* uses the whole dividend to buy a non-renewable, one-year term addition that will be paid if the life insured dies during that year.

Dividends Used to Reduce Premiums:

When dividends are used to reduce the outlay of the policy owner for premiums, it is called premium offset. The simplest method for you to reduce premiums using dividends from a participating policy is to apply the cash you receive to the premium payment. There is a benefit and a disadvantage to choosing this course of action. The benefit is that you reduce your outlay towards the premium. For instance, when the annual premium is $3,200 and you receive $200 in dividends, the premium is reduced by the dividends to $3,000 ($3,200 - $200).

The disadvantage of premium offset is that you are not acquiring more life insurance via additions.

Paid-up additions (PUAs), as discussed above, can be purchased with dividends. You may choose to reduce premiums by using the dividends of the PUAs or cashing in individual PUAs. Thus, if the annual premium is $3,200, and you have reinvested dividends each year in a PUA, you might receive $100 in dividends from PUAs. You could use the $100 against the $3,200 premium to reduce the premium to $3,100 ($3,200 - $100). In addition, you might choose to sacrifice a single PUA, receive its cash surrender value ($100), and use the $100 towards the premium, so that the premium is then reduced to $3,000 ($3,100 - $100). Thus, the premium is reduced by a combination of PUA dividends and/or PUA cash surrender value.

As when dividends are used as a cash equivalent, you reduce your outlay towards premiums by using PUAs. However, when PUAs are used, the policy reserve of the underlying policy is not increased, as it would be by premiums you have paid. Thus, the policy reserve will not increase over time and the CSV will be lower.

Universal Life Insurance

Universal life insurance is a unique combination of insurance and investment that offers flexibility unlike any other type of life insurance while still offering estate protection.

The universal life policy is often referred to as an account; this reflects the investment nature of the policy.

We have already discussed how a whole life policy builds a policy reserve from overpayment of premiums in the early years of the policy. Universal life may also build a reserve from the investment account or accounts that comprise a part of the policy. The management of the investment account is in your hands as the policy owner. The account value of the universal life policy is the total of all the investments in the investment account less deductions for the current month's expenses.

How to invest the account value is just one of the decisions required by a universal life policy owner. You must also choose between how premiums will be structured and death benefit options. Together, these choices allow you to tailor the policy to meet your needs.

One of the key features of universal life is its flexibility. You can increase or decrease the **face amount** of the insurance with satisfactory evidence of insurability, add more lives to be insured under the policy, and substitute one life insured for another. The amount and duration of the **premiums** and how the savings are **invested** are also highly flexible.

Whole life policy owners receive the cash value of their policy if it is surrendered. On death, they receive the death benefit.

Therefore, they receive the cash value or the death benefit.

Universal life policy owners can choose to receive the cash value of their policy in addition to the death benefit.

There are three separate parts to a universal policy — **insurance**, **investment**, and **expenses**. Unlike other types of policies, where the factors that determine the price of the policy are not revealed to the policy owner, a universal life policy lists separately the cost of insurance (the mortality charge applied to the policy), the interest rate applied to the account value of the policy, and the expense charges of the insurer (for administration, expenses, and sales costs) as they apply to the policy.

The insurance component of universal life

The cost for insurance protection in a universal life policy is called the mortality charge. It is based on:

- the age of the insured;
- the risk classification of the insured that is based on gender, smoking status, health factors, etc.;
- the face amount of the policy;
- the cost of insurance based on the net amount at risk.

When the policy is issued, you must choose whether the life insurance coverage will be based on a yearly term rate (that will increase annually; based on yearly renewable term [YRT] rates) or a level term rate (that will remain constant, or *level*, for life; based on term-to-100 [T-100] rates and called the level cost of insurance [LCOI]). The cost for insurance is deducted from your account monthly.

The choice between the two rates should be made with care: each has special considerations. YRT premiums will be low initially, but, as the insured ages, premiums will escalate. T-100 premiums may be higher initially, but will remain constant over time. The cash values in each policy also accumulate at different rates.

Deposits into the universal life policy build a pool of savings in the account, called the **account value**, or the **accumulation fund**. As long as the account value can pay the mortality charge and policy expenses, there is no need for premium payments by the policy owner.

The minimum premium is designed to keep the policy in force to age 100. There is a maximum premium allowable; it is defined by a formula in the *Income Tax Act*. If the maximum is exceeded, the policy loses its tax status as an insurance policy and is subject to tax as an investment that must be reported annually.

Unique to universal life, you have the option of having premiums *increased* or *decreased*, based on minimum requirements and maximums allowed, or they can be stopped and restarted, if the account value can pay the cost of insurance and expenses.

If you fail to maintain enough funds in the account to pay the mortality charge and expenses, the insurer gives you a period of time, at least 30 days, to make a premium payment to cover the shortfall. If you fail to pay these charges, the policy will lapse.

The expense component of universal life

Expense charges against the universal-life policy include administration, expenses, and sales costs. They are deducted from the account monthly.

The investment component of universal life

Premiums and deposits made to the account are invested by the policy owner in products offered by the insurer. There are many products from which to choose, including savings accounts, guaranteed term deposits, investment funds, and segregated funds.

The investment earnings that grow within the account are credited as "interest income." The interest income within a universal life policy does not have to be declared each year, allowing you to benefit from compounding returns and deferral of taxes.

An account need not be entirely guaranteed (safely invested) or entirely non-guaranteed (risky investments); a balanced portfolio holds both types of investments.

Fundamentally, universal life policies offer two basic investment options: one investment option guarantees the rate of return, such as would be received in a daily interest account, Guaranteed Investment Certificates, or Treasury Bills; the other investment option provides no guarantees. Instead, investments fluctuate in relation to market performance by linking to market indexes or a vast array of mutual funds or mutual-fund portfolios.

Features of universal life similar to whole life

Like whole life insurance, universal life offers:

- a cash surrender value (CSV);
- policy loans;
- premium offset.

Cash Surrender Value:

The cash surrender value of the policy is determined by the total account value. The total account value is the total of all the investments in the investment account, less deductions for the current month's expenses. The CSV is the total account value minus outstanding loans minus surrender charges. Many policies have a surrender charge that applies if the policy is surrendered. These may apply up to 20 years after the policy was issued.

Policy Loans:

A universal life policy loan is usually available. The amount borrowed cannot exceed the cash surrender value of the account. There will be a tax implication if the loan exceeds the adjusted cost basis (ACB) of the policy. If the life insured dies with an outstanding policy loan, death benefits will be reduced by the amount remaining on the loan, plus interest.

Premium Offset:

The need for future premiums can be eliminated by paying larger than required premiums in the early years of the policy. The premiums are paid by the accumulated tax-sheltered investments in the account.

Unique features of universal life

The ability of the policy owner to make a cash withdrawal from the account value of the policy without forfeiting the policy is unique to universal life, as is the ability to select from a number of settlement options on death.

Cash Withdrawal:

Universal life policies provide the policy owner with the option to make a cash withdrawal from the policy. This withdrawal, called a partial surrender, does not have to be repaid. If not repaid, it will reduce the amount of the death benefit. There are however tax implications to a withdrawal.

Universal life insurance is the only life insurance that allows the policy owner to make a withdrawal from the policy.

Death Benefit Choices:

Universal life provides a variety of death benefits to reflect the nature of the policy as insurance and as an investment. Usually the policy owner considers the needs of the beneficiary first. Other facts to be weighed include your investment objectives, your ability to pay premiums, and personal preferences.

Review

As you can see, permanent insurance offers much more than estate-planning security; its cash values allow you to consider its use to supplement retirement income or to access cash for emergencies. It is essential for you to discuss your personal needs and objectives with your life agent.

Wrap-Up

It is uncomfortable to contemplate the end of life, and people generally avoid unpleasant or uncomfortable tasks. This certainly must be the reason why so many people fail to prepare a will. But preparing for the time when you are no longer alive is simply being practical; you are exercising a measure of control by taking affairs into your own hands instead of deferring difficult decisions to others.

You should see by now that estate planning is not half as intimidating as you once thought. Congratulations! This knowledge puts you far ahead of many people who are too afraid even to begin thinking about what should be done, to more or less take charge of the task.

It should surely also be evident from reading this book that estate planning is not something that you can—or should—do on your own. Your first activity is going to be putting together your personal estate-planning team: your lawyer, your executor, your power of attorney, your accountant, your life insurance agent, your banker or investment advisor, and even possibly someone to chip in on some of the ethical issues you will face—this could be your pastor, your yogi, or your best friend. Make sure they know that your reason to connect with them is the development of the estate plan. Each member of the team will contribute their expertise to the benefit of the whole; each will have questions for you that may challenge your beliefs and provide you with yet more information that you must assimilate.

To begin, you need to find all those documents that have a bearing upon the value of your estate, including your will, your mortgage, your investment statements, and your insurance policy, and also those that pertain to your debts. Make a list of all items of personal property that you wish to bequeath—from the valuable, like your collection of sterling silver, to the sentimental, such as old photographs. Note who is to receive what.

Who is to receive what is one of the biggest and most difficult of the estate-planning issues. Adult children can be especially sensitive to being slighted, or to the perception that they are being slighted, by a parent who leaves "more" to one or some than to others. Whether they are correct or not, inequality of inheritance can leave broken hearts, feuding siblings, and never-ending bitterness.

Take the bull by the horns and have the conversation about your plans with all those who stand to benefit—while you're alive and well. Listen to their feedback. More than one meeting may be required to ensure that all will finally be squared away and you can enjoy the peace of mind that will come from having aligned your brood and their expectations with your wishes.

Finally, remember that expectations change over time. This will be true of your expectations, and those of the people who stand to benefit from your estate. In the years that may elapse after the time that you feel you have things "squared away," you may have many changes in your life that you want to acknowledge. It is not unusual for people, as they age, to think more seriously about leaving a public legacy, whether to a charitable institution, an arts organization, or a hospital that has provided exemplary services. This may not have occurred to them even five years earlier. It's never too late to make a change, providing your team of experts and family members is made aware of your wishes and the reasons for them.

Now, only one step remains: get started!

Appendix 1: HOW LONG SHOULD I PLAN FOR?

	Male				Female			
Your Age Now	Your Probability of Survival to Age ______							
	40%	30%	20%	10%	40%	30%	20%	10%
20-45	81	84	87	91	87	89	92	96
50	81	84	87	91	87	90	92	96
55	82	84	87	91	87	90	92	96
60	82	85	88	91	87	90	93	96
65	83	85	88	92	88	90	93	96
70	84	86	89	92	88	91	93	96

Source: Statistics Canada

For many people leaving an estate is not realistic, whereas future rates of return on annuities are uncertain. If this applies to you, your best option might be to time your retirement savings to gradually deplete till the end of life. For those who make this choice and, to a lesser extent, also for those who must anticipate their post-retirement spending in a retirement budget, which may change over time, a mandatory component of the time value of money calculation is N—i.e., the number of years remaining till the end of life. Failure to tackle this question realistically raises the spectre of outliving one's money, which can result in impoverishment or worse at the very end of life, when one is most vulnerable. With the doubling of medical knowledge every ten years, many people are living longer. Many people grossly underestimate their life expectancy. Statistical averages are also misleading, since 50% of the population will outlive their statistical average life expectancy for at least some period of time.

The best single predictor of longevity is one's current age. The table above shows the life expectancy of 40%, 30%, 20% and 10% of the Canadian population between the ages of 20 and 70. The reliability of a retirement plan will inversely correlate with the probability of survival, and should certainly not be less than 70%., i.e., the 30% survival column. If one uses this column for planning there is a 1 in 3 probability of outliving one's money for at least some period of time. The 20% to 10% survival columns, corresponding to 80% and 90% reliability respectively, represent higher degrees of certainty. A 100% reliable plan will of course assume the genetically maximum life expectancy of 115 to 120 years, but will also be significantly more expensive.

To use the mortality calculator above for planning purposes, find your current age and gender and try to design your personal financial plan around one of the ages in the shaded area for 80% to 90% reliability, unless you have strong specific reasons to think that these statistical averages may not apply to you. If in doubt, you should also discuss the matter with your doctor.

Appendix 2: HOW MUCH LIFE INSURANCE DO I NEED?

1. In the event of my death, what immediate expenses will be incurred? *(Note: Only include one-time liabilities that will be paid off immediately.)*

Education fund	
Emergency fund	
Funeral and burial/cremation expense	
Pay off car loan	
Pay off debt/taxes	
Pay off mortgage	
Probate, legal and administrative fees (est.)	
Transitional expenses for survivor	
(A) TOTAL CASH NEEDED AT DEATH	

2. In the event of my death, what liquid assets will be immediately available? *(Note: Only include assets of the estate that will be received or liquidated at or shortly after death, after deducting any commissions, taxes, or other associated expenses.)*

Cash or near-cash (e.g., T-bills, CSBs, etc.)	
Death benefits – CPP/QPP	
Death benefits – RPP	
Investment portfolio	
Life insurance - group	
Life insurance - personal	
Real estate	
RRSP assets	
Any other assets to be liquidated	
(B) TOTAL LIQUID ASSETS AT DEATH	

How much extra cash will be required at death? (A – B)

(C) ______________

3. In the event of my death, how much extra long-term income will be required by my survivor(s) (*if any*)?

	PER MONTH	PER YEAR
Lost income/required income (e.g., 70–80% of current income)		
(MINUS: Survivor's benefits)		
(MINUS: Childrens' benefits)		
NET ADDITIONAL INCOME REQUIRED		
(DIVIDED BY: Assumed Rate of Return on Capital, e.g., 4% or 5%)		

TOTAL ADDITIONAL CAPITAL REQUIRED

(D) ______________

(Note: This calculation assumes indefinite continuation of the required nominal income. The capital needed may be reduced by assuming a limited term and depletion to zero over the course of the term. This calculation requires the use of a financial calculator. The assumed rate of return on capital may or may not be adjusted for inflation.)

TOTAL LIFE INSURANCE REQUIRED (C + D)

(if result is negative, no more insurance is needed)

Glossary

The Financial Literacy You Need

To understand the subject, you need to know the lingo. These are the terms you should know in order to communicate effectively with your life agent:

Adjusted Cost Base (ACB)

Used in the calculation of capital gains. The proceeds of disposition (the sale price), minus any selling expenses, minus the adjusted cost base will equal the capital gain. In most cases, the adjusted cost base is simply the cost of the property.

Adjusted Cost Basis (ACB)

Used in the calculation of the cost of a life insurance policy; it is typically the amount paid in premiums.

Alter-Ego or Joint-Partner Trusts

These are special types of inter vivos (living) trusts, whereby a person can transfer assets under certain conditions, and a choice can be made to pay tax on the assets transferred, or defer the tax until the death of the person or of the surviving partner (i.e. spouse, common-law spouse, or same-sex partner in the case of a joint-partner trust).

Alternative executor

This is an executor who is named in the will as a contingency if the original executor dies or declines to act or cannot act.

Annuity

This is a contract between a person and the issuer. The person pays the issuer a premium and the issuer makes regular payments to the person. These payments may be fixed or variable.

Beneficiary(ies)

The person or persons who receive the deceased person's assets or life insurance death benefit.

Capital gain

The gain that results when a capital property (asset) is sold for more than its adjusted cost base.

Capital loss

The loss that results when a capital property (asset) is sold for less than its adjusted cost base.

Capital property

This is property that, when disposed of, will result in a capital gain or loss.

Charitable remainder trusts

A type of inter vivos (living) trust whereby assets are irrevocably transferred to the trust. The income generated by the trust is paid to the settlor (see below) and/or spouse of the settlor, for life. On their deaths, the trust is wound up, and a charity designated as the beneficiary receives the remainder of the trust assets.

Charitable trust

Set up with the purpose of benefiting either the public or a community.

Codicil

This is a document or letter, signed or validated like a will, that amends the will by revoking, adding, or revising clauses.

Co-Executor

In a will, more than one executor may be named and all must agree on the decisions to be made (unless the will provides otherwise).

Contingent beneficiary

In an insurance policy, if the primary beneficiary dies before the insured, the contingent beneficiary is the next person who would receive the benefits of that policy.

Deemed disposition

Certain events that affect a person (e.g., death), or certain actions taken by a person (e.g., a non-arm's-length transfer), trigger a deemed disposition of that person's capital property. This means that, for tax purposes, a capital gain is triggered as if his or her capital property has been sold for its current market value, thus triggering a capital gain on all increases that have accrued on the property since it was purchased.

Deductible

An insurance policy may contain a provision whereby the insured is responsible for any losses up to a certain dollar limit, in return for a lower premium.

Dividend

A per-share payment, designated by a company's board of directors, that is distributed among shareholders. For preferred shares, the dividend is generally a fixed amount. For common shares, the dividend varies with the fortunes of the company and the amount of cash on hand. In the case of life insurance, the dividend payment made to a participating permanent life insurance policyowner is a refund of premium overpayment.

Estate freeze

An estate freeze is designed to freeze the value of a taxpayer's "growth assets" so that future asset growth passes to the taxpayer's family members. Growth assets consist of quoted shares, bonds, and property.

Executor

A personal representative, appointed under a will, whose primary responsibility is to distribute a testator's assets according to the instructions set out in the will. When there is a continuing trust established by a will, an executor can also be known as a trustee.

Holograph will

This is a form of a will that is written by hand and signed by the testator.

In-Kind donations

These are charitable donations that include capital and depreciating property, insurance policies, securities, rights (e.g., royalties), etc.

International will

A will made in a country that complies with the convention that allows international wills. They are valid in every country that has a reciprocal convention, regardless of the domicile of the testator where the will was executed or the location of the testator's assets.

Inter-Vivos (Living) trusts

These trusts are set up during one's lifetime. They can also be called family trusts or personal trusts.

Intestate

To die intestate means to die without having made a will.

Investment discretion clause

An optional clause for a will. Under the relevant trustee act, an executor may be restricted to making only conservative investments—which often have low yields—for the estate. If this clause is inserted, it gives the executor greater investment discretion.

Investment income

This income consists of interest, taxable dividends, and other income from investment assets such as capital gains.

Joint tenancy

When two or more individuals own land subject to certain rights. When one individual dies, his or her ownership interest transfers to the survivor(s) of the tenancy, i.e., the other partner(s).

Living wills

Also called advance health-care directives, they can include a power of attorney, and instruct medical practitioners about the nature and intensity of medical treatment that the person wishes to receive.

Multiple wills

This means that two separate wills are drawn up, each with its own executor. The primary will is used to distribute probatable assets only, while the secondary will is used to distribute assets which do not require probate. Valid only in Ontario.

Per capita basis

When a person leaves an inheritance to children on a per capita basis, each child must be alive at the death of the testator to inherit.

Per stirpes basis

When a person leaves an inheritance to children on a per stirpes basis, then the grandchildren will inherit the portion of the estate that their parent would have received if he or she had not predeceased the testator.

Planned gifts

These are charitable donation that are designed and timed to maximize tax savings (e.g., non-refundable tax credits).

Probate

This is the judicial process to confirm that a will is valid and that an executor(s) has been appointed. It is the official indication that a will is genuine.

Registered Pension Plan (RPP)

A trust that is registered with Canada Revenue Agency and established by a company to provide retirement pension benefits for its employees.

Registered Retirement Savings Plans (RRSPs)

These are individual retirement savings plans that have been registered with Canada Customs and Revenue Agency. They permit tax-deductible contributions to the plan, and any income earned in the plan is exempt from tax until payments from the plan are received.

Settlor of a trust

A person who creates and contributes assets to a trust.

Spousal trust

This is a type of trust wherein the spouse is the sole beneficiary.

Tax credit

A direct reduction in tax liability (regardless of tax bracket).

Tax deduction

Also known as a writeoff, this reduces the taxable income on which your federal tax is calculated. An RRSP contribution of $1,000 is worth more in tax savings to an individual in a higher tax bracket than one in a lower tax bracket.

Testamentary trust

These trusts are created by a will to manage assets on behalf of named beneficiaries.

Testator

A person who makes a will.

Term insurance

Insurance taken out for a certain period of time. If the insured dies before the policy expires, the insurance company will pay the beneficiary. If a policy ends and the insured is still alive, coverage ceases.

Trust

A trust is created when one party (the settlor) transfers assets to another party who holds the legal title (the trustee), with instructions as to how the assets are to be used for the benefit of certain parties (the beneficiaries).

Universal-life insurance

This is an insurance policy that consists of two parts: term insurance and an investment account. A portion of each premium goes towards the insurance coverage, and the balance is credited to an investment account. Premiums can be increased or decreased, and be paid when due or on unscheduled dates, as long as there is sufficient cash value to cover mortality costs. Death benefits can be increased within certain limits. In addition to death benefits being tax sheltered, some investment income is tax sheltered. The policy owner decides what to do with the investment income and death benefit component.

Whole-life insurance

This is an insurance policy that is in force for the lifetime of the life-insured; it can be structured to pay dividends (called a participating or par policy) or not (called a non-participating or non-par policy). The payment of premiums to the policy builds a cash value that can be accessed for policy loans and other options, called non-forfeiture options. If the policy is surrendered, the policy owner will receive the cash surrender value (CSV) of the policy.

Index

ORDER FORM

Please send me:

____ copy/copies of Estate Planning, Life Insurance and Taxes for Canadians @ $19.95/copy $________

____ copy/copies of Retirement Planning and Taxes for Canadians @ $19.95/copy $________

____ copy/copies of Investing for Retirement and Taxes for Canadians @ $19.95/copy $________

Subtotal	$________
GST @ 5%	$________
Shipping and handling	$________
Total price	$________

Special Pricing: Order any two books @$34.95 or $49.95 for all three (plus GST and $5.95 shipping and handling)

Method of Payment:

❑ cheque enclosed (made payable to Oliver Publishing)

❑ credit card:

- ❑ VISA
- ❑ Mastercard
- ❑ American Express

Number on card: ____________________

Expiry date: _____ / _____ /

Shipping Address:

Name: ____________________

Address 1: ____________________

Address 2: ____________________

City/Town: ____________________

Province: ____________________

Postal code: ____________________

❑ Is this a gift? Name on gift enclosure:

To: ____________________

From: ____________________

Message: ____________________

____

Send to:

Oliver Publishing, 151 Bloor Street West, Suite 800, Toronto, ON M5S 1S4